PRAISE FOR *NO MORE PERFECT MOMS*

No More Perfect Moms is a **must-read survival manual for moms of all ages**. Jill Savage talks straight about how an imaginary mom with a clean house, ideal husband, model kids, and no problems or struggles doesn't really exist. Jill transparently shares practical tips on how to respond right to difficult situations and how to make your home a Christ-honoring haven for your family!

—MICHELLE DUGGAR, *mother of 19 kids and counting*

Every day at Focus on the Family we hear from moms who love what they're doing, and yet they're burned out. Jill Savage understands that frustration because she's been there. **I wish every mom could read *No More Perfect Moms*—it's a book full of wisdom, humor, and grace.**

—JIM DALY, *president, Focus on the Family*

Jill gives me permission to be exactly who I am . . . an imperfect woman, wife, and mom perfectly accepted by God. **This is a timely message that goes straight to the need of a woman's heart.** Jill's message will help free the woman bound by perfectionism while at the same time prevent young women from catching the Perfection Infection!

—JENNIFER ROTHSCHILD, *author including* Lessons I Learned in the Dark *and* Me, Myself and Lies, *founder of Fresh Grounded Faith Conferences and WomensMinistry.net*

As I read No More Perfect Moms a weight lifted from my weary shoulders. I've been doing this mom thing for 24 years—yet once again I'm a mom to a toddler—and I still wish I could be "more perfect on so many levels." With encouraging, gentle words Jill Savage lowered the "noise" of the worry, guilt, and expectations, allowing me to tune in to my Savior's whisper, "*I love you. I have a good plan for you and your kids. I'm here.*"

—TRICIA GOYER, *bestselling author of 35 books*

Dear Reader, before opening the pages of this **"best ever" book from Jill Savage,** you must ask yourself if you are ready to get up close and personal with who you are as a mom, wife, sister, woman, and daughter! This book will scrub you like a wonderful sugar scrub! Jill's writing is REAL and has no room for masks as she encourages and challenges you to be all that you are created to be in each of your uniquely, amazing roles!

—YVETTE MAHER, *executive pastor, New Life Church*

Dance! Spin around with joy! Jill Savage provides the antidote to the Perfection Infection so that **moms everywhere can parent their children free from impossible expectations**. You'll treasure Jill's warmth and honesty as she shares personally from her own imperfect world. Join the mom movement gathering momentum around the country to ban the word "perfection" from the parenting dictionary.

—LORRAINE PINTUS, *author, including* Jump Off the Hormone Swing, *speaker, and writing coach*

Imperfect moms: Unite! For every mother who forgot to pick her son up after soccer practice, made a lunch out of cheese sticks and pudding packs, or did drive-thru five nights in a row for dinner, you have found a friend. With warmth, grace, and been-there-blew-that parenting stories, Jill Savage leads all of us imperfect moms into the loving space of our perfect God. So put aside your unfinished baby albums and pick up this book. You'll be relieved to know that there is hope for all of us less-than-perfect parents.

—KATHI LIPP, *speaker and author, including* The Husband Project

Wow. This book should be handed to every mother along with her first child! As a seasoned mom, I found myself in every chapter, wondering if Jill had literally been hiding in my pantry and taking notes! From start to finish, Jill Savage's *No More Perfect Moms* is timely, practical, and the perfect prescription for every mom who struggles with feeling "less than."
Jill's insight into the disease of Perfection Infection is something every mom needs to hear. Her personal examples are humbling, and her empathy is palpable, as she bravely and compassionately points the way to grace. I long to live in a world where we as moms embrace one another "as is," yet strive to help one another be everything God has called us and our families to be.
I thought I was a pretty "what-you-see-is-what-you-get" mom, but **No More Perfect Moms has challenged me to new levels of authenticity**. Thank you Jill, for giving us moms permission to be a work in progress.

—SALLY BAUCKE, *speaker, comedienne, funnygalsal.com*

NO MORE PERFECT MOMS

Learn to Love Your Real Life

JILL SAVAGE

MOODY PUBLISHERS
CHICAGO

All scripture quotations, unless otherwise indicated, are taken from the *Holy Bible, New International Version*®, NIV®. Copyright ©1973, 1978, 1984, 2011 by Biblica, Inc.™ Used by permission of Zondervan. All rights reserved worldwide. www.zondervan.com.

Scripture quotations marked NLT are taken from the *Holy Bible, New Living Translation*, copyright © 1996, 2004. Used by permission of Tyndale House Publishers, Inc., Wheaton, Illinois 60189, U.S.A. All rights reserved.

Scripture quotations marked ESV are taken from *The Holy Bible, English Standard Version*. Copyright © 2000, 2001 by Crossway Bibles, a division of Good News Publishers. Used by permission. All rights reserved.

Edited by Annette LaPlaca
Cover design: Faceout Studio
Cover image: Getty / 145073689
Interior design: Smartt Guys design

Library of Congress Cataloging-in-Publication Data

Savage, Jill, 1964-
No more perfect moms : learn to love your real life / Jill Savage.
    pages cm
Includes bibliographical references.
ISBN 978-0-8024-0637-8
1. Motherhood–Religious aspects–Christianity. 2. Mothers–Religious life. I. Title.
BV4529.18.S247 2013
248.8'431–dc23

                    2012044200

All websites and phone numbers listed herein are accurate at the time of publication, but may change in the future or cease to exist. The listing of website references and resources does not imply publisher endorsement of the site's entire contents. Groups and organizations are listed for informational purposes, and listing does not imply publisher endorsement of their activities.

We hope you enjoy this book from Moody Publishers. Our goal is to provide high-quality, thought-provoking books and products that connect truth to your real needs and challenges. For more information on other books and products written and produced from a biblical perspective, go to www.moodypublishers.com or write to:

Moody Publishers
820 N. LaSalle Boulevard
Chicago, IL 60610

5 7 9 10 8 6

Printed in the United States of America

To my daughters, Anne and Erica:

*May your mothering journey be filled with love, grace,
and the freedom of authenticity*

CONTENTS

Introduction

*I*t seems appropriate that I'm writing the introduction for this book today. It's my daughter's first day of being a mother of two. I had the privilege of watching Landon William McClane come into this world less than twenty-four hours ago.

Adding a child into a family, whether by birth or by adoption, comes with hopes, dreams, and our best intentions as a mother. I've experienced that five times, four by birth and once by adoption. With each addition I renewed my desire to be the best mom I could be. I wanted to give each child the greatest opportunities. I dreamed about who that child would become. I hoped for that child's future.

And then reality set in.

When child number one threw a fit in the grocery store, screaming at the top of her lungs in this very public place, I was so embarrassed. When I'd witnessed a scene like that *before* I had children, I swore my own kids would never do that. When my teenage son sneaked out of the house one night and I had a police officer knock on my door at 3 a.m., I couldn't believe one of *my* kids had done such a thing. The truth is now that I'm a mom, I find myself in all kinds of situations I never thought I'd experience.

Inside I begin to think, "What's wrong with me?"

Kids don't sleep much, and too often I've found myself beyond weary. Mine didn't potty train as quickly as other kids the same age. As my teens grew older and began to have minds of their own, they were often quite sure they knew more than I did.

I'm less patient than I thought I'd be. I weigh more than I want. My children are more strong-willed than I expected. My house seems to always be a mess. At times, my marriage isn't the "happily ever after" I dreamed it would be.

Inside I begin to think thoughts like, *I don't measure up. I'm failing as a mom. My kids don't act like* her *kids. My house doesn't look like* her *house. My body doesn't look like* her *body. My husband doesn't help like* her *husband does. What is wrong with me?*

Have you ever felt that way? Have you wondered what is wrong with you, with your family, with your kids?

Nothing is wrong with you or your family. You are normal. Your frustrations are normal. Your disappointments are normal. Your struggles are normal. In fact, that's what this book is all about: the reassurance that you are normal.

There are no perfect moms (just women who make a good outward appearance). There are no perfect kids (just kids who are dressed well and behave well just when you see them). There are no perfect houses (just ones where the clutter is cleverly stored!). There are no perfect bodies (just ones that have discovered the beauty of Spanx!).

While we're pursuing perfection, we're missing out on the most precious parts of life.

Perfection doesn't exist—but unfortunately we waste a lot of time and energy pursuing the elusive mirage we're just sure can be found. While we're pursuing perfection, we're missing out on the most precious parts of life: the laughter of silliness, the joy of spontaneity, the lessons found in failure, and the freedom found in grace.

Let's take a journey together to find the realities of "normal." Let's stop trying to find "perfect" and embrace "authentic." Let's hear some real stories about real moms. Turn the page with me; I think you'll find you are not as alone as you sometimes think you are.

CHAPTER 1

THE *Perfection* INFECTION

*T*he phone rang in the chaos of the "after-school-almost dinner-time" hour. I was making a dinner salad (translated: I poured a bag of lettuce into a pretty glass bowl and threw some cherry tomatoes on for color!), helping two kids with their homework, and trying to keep my four-year-old busy enough not to whine for dinner.

I grabbed the phone and shoved it between my ear and my shoulder, answering with a quick, "Hello, this is Jill!" The voice on the other end of the line was obviously emotional. "Mom, this is Erica. Did you forget me?"

I quickly did a head count: one, two, three . . . four—oh my. *Erica's not here. I thought all my chicks were in the nest, but there was one at basketball practice, and it completely slipped my mind that she wasn't*

. . . .

home and I needed to pick her up!

I couldn't lie. "Erica, I am so sorry!" I apologized. "I completely forgot to pick you up. I will be right there!"

The sniffling on the other end of the phone made my guilt run deeper. *How could I forget my own child? What kind of mom does something like that? How will she ever forgive me?*

Welcome to real life! If we're honest with one another, we all have stories like that to share. There are no perfect moms.

INSIDES AND OUTSIDES

Like most moms, I entered the motherhood scene wanting to be the perfect mom. I read. I prepared. I planned. I dreamed. I determined to be intentional about everything I did from choosing the laundry detergent that would be best for their skin to choosing the school that would be best for their education. I was going to be supermom. I would do it all and do it all well. Then life happened.

My pursuit of being the "perfect mom" set me up for failure from day one.

People often say, "Hindsight is 20/20." Looking back on that late-afternoon scene now, eleven years later, I have a valuable perspective I didn't have then. My daughter Erica, who is now twenty-one, isn't emotionally scarred because I forgot her at basketball practice. She's a well-adjusted young adult who has a great story to tell, especially when she wants to get a little sympathy or a good laugh at family gatherings.

I now understand that my pursuit of being the "perfect mom" set me up for failure from day one. There are no perfect moms—just imperfect women who will fall off the pedestal of their own expectations more often than they care to admit.

. . . .

A good friend once told me, "Jill, never compare your insides to someone else's outsides." She shared that wisdom when she heard me unconsciously compare myself to another mom after one of my many failures. That powerful statement still sticks with me. I now realize that most moms play the comparison game dozens of times every day. We constantly look to see how we measure up to those around us. And we *don't* measure up. But how can we measure up? We compare ourselves to something that doesn't exist. We compare our messy insides—our struggles, our failures, our less-than-perfect lives—to other women's carefully cleaned-up, perfect-looking outsides. It's a game we moms play that we can never ever win.

So if we insist on playing the comparison game (and most of us do!), then it's time for a new measuring stick. Instead of comparing insides to outsides, we need to compare insides to insides. In fact, that's what I hope to do by sharing honestly in the coming pages.

If we're honest, too many of us wear motherhood masks that keep our insides from peeking out. Sometimes those masks are based on outward appearance. We wear fashionable clothes and never leave the house without our makeup done and our hair styled. In other words, on the outside we always look like we have it together. Others of us wear a mask in our conversations with other moms. We would never admit we are struggling in any way, even if others are openly talking about their struggles. Some of us wear masks of pride. We only share the good and never talk about the bad. We pretend we're more confident than we really are.

Authors Justin and Trisha Davis talk further about masks.

We wear masks at church. We argue all the way to Sunday service and paint on a smile on our way in. We pretend to be more spiritual, more put together, more mature in our faith than we really are. We fear that if anyone knew the real us, they would think less of us . . . so we mask our brokenness.

We wear masks at home. We pretend things are okay in our marriage when there is distance. We say nothing is wrong when our feelings are truly hurt. We don't necessarily lie to our spouse; we just shade part of the truth. We don't feel comfortable being our true self with our spouse because we are afraid of judgment or ridicule.

The thing about masks is that they never bring us closer to who we were created to be. Masks always make shallow what God has intended to be deep. Friendships. Marriages. Families. Churches. Everything in our lives get cheated when we choose to be fake.[1]

Would you like to live a grace-filled life that loves instead of judges?

Have you ever thought about the fact that you are cheating yourself by wearing a mask? Have you ever considered that fake smile is keeping you from the depth of relationships you're really longing for?

I'd like to put "being fake" away for good in the journey of motherhood. Masks do not serve us well. They keep us at an arm's length from our friends, our family, and our God. Not only that, but wearing masks breeds judgment. It keeps us judging ourselves and others instead of living in and loving through grace.

Are you ready for a new lens through which to view life? Would you like to live a grace-filled life that loves instead of judges? Would you like to leave perfectionism behind and find freedom in authenticity? I know I would!

So where do we start? To understand where we are and where we need to go, it's wise to start with a sense of how we got here. Let's explore this: Just how did our lives become so infected with perfectionism?

HOW DID WE GET HERE?

I noticed it for the first time just a couple of years ago. There was a little box I could check on my boys' school picture order form if I'd like the photographer to provide "touch up services" for their school pictures. You know: remove a zit here, fix an out-of-place hair there. Many of us no longer want a "real" picture of who our kids are. We want them to look better than they really do. Given the option, we choose to remove their "imperfections" because we're not okay with anything less than perfect. After all, we're comparing ourselves — and our kids — to those around us.

The temptation to compare ourselves to others goes all the way back to Adam and Eve. Adam and Eve were two people in the most perfect setting. No worries. All of their needs provided for.

Satan came along and started feeding them lies about themselves and about God. They compared their situation to his lies and decided that life in the garden wasn't all it was cracked up to be. They acted on impulse and broke the only rule God had given them — not to eat of just one tree in the garden. Despite their perfect existence, Adam and Eve still felt the need for something else, something more. Their children carried on the comparison game when Cain killed Abel out of jealousy. And the saga continues: Story after story in the Bible illustrates that people have always played the comparison game.

. . . .

So it's human nature to compare, to be discontent, and to want something different from what we have. But what has driven us to try to attain something as unattainable as perfection? The culprit is in front of our faces every day.

Our generation of mothers is more socially connected than any previous generation. The explosion of media in the past fifty years and social media in the past ten years has connected us to so many more people to whom we compare ourselves. Think about it: all you and I have to do is stand in the checkout aisle at WalMart and we are assaulted by the headlines, "Lose 30 lbs. in 30 days!" "Meet Brad and Angelina's Perfect Family!" We see pictures of "perfect" houses, "perfect" bodies, and "perfect" families splashed on the front of the magazines we walk by as we pay for our groceries. The hard part of this comparison game is that we aren't comparing ourselves to reality. The photos are Photoshopped and airbrushed, the stories are edited, and the guarantee of perfection is overpromised in order to sell magazines.

More than ten years ago, I personally had the privilege of being on the cover of a Christian magazine. What an experience! A photo shoot, several outfit changes, a makeup artist—wow! I could never have dreamed I'd get to experience something like that. Imagine my surprise when I discovered that my photos had been edited: a little removal of a blemish here, airbrush the skin there. That's right, even in the Christian media, we've fallen prey to presenting perfection. After all, our culture demands it.

When you see a picture of a kitchen makeover in a magazine, remember those pictures are staged. That's not how that kitchen will look when someone cooks in it. Then there will be crumbs on the counter, something sticky on the floor, and a sink full of dirty dishes that need to be washed. When you see a picture of a family playing together in a magazine, on a billboard, or in an advertisement, remember the picture is set up to create a certain feeling—and those people in the picture probably aren't even related. It's even possible these actors argued with their real spouses before they left the house or are dealing with financial issues in their personal life. When you see pictures of a movie star who has slimmed down to her pre-pregnancy weight just three months after giving birth, remember she's not only likely had a personal trainer and a chef, but the photos have probably been retouched to give an illusion of perfection.

While magazines give us unrealistic visual pictures against which to compare our real bodies and our real homes, we can thank Hollywood for painting unrealistic relational pictures for us. Every sitcom presents and resolves some kind of problem in a thirty-minute time span. Every movie presents some event or season of life that gets tidily wrapped up within a mere two hours. Sure they show conflict or even messy relational challenges, but usually the good guy wins and the bad guy gets his deserved justice by the end of the show. Even the reality shows aren't real. They have been cut and edited so much that they sometimes misrepresent what really happened in a scene.

Facebook, Twitter, and Pinterest can be culprits, too! As we look at the status someone posts, we think, *I wish my kid would say something cute like that.* Or *I wish I could say something nice like that about my husband.* On Pinterest, we can find ourselves wishing we had more creativity or better ideas as we look at all the great organizational tools or craft projects people share.

·········

The more we compare, the higher our expectations are set and the more the Perfection Infection sets in. Without realizing it, we want our problems to be solved in thirty minutes to two hours. Unconsciously, we long for our skin to look like the model in that commercial we just watched. Instinctively, we long for a pretty house with flowers on the counter and no toys strewn across the floor. Our expectations are fueled by a constant barrage of "perfect" scenes and images we see in our media-saturated society.

Not only does this increase our desire for a perfect house, perfect kids, a perfect body, and a perfect husband, it actually causes us to be discontent with our real houses, our real kids, our real bodies, and our real husbands. Even worse, most of the time we don't even realize that's what we are doing. It's a subtle erosion of our satisfaction. If we don't recognize it, the discontentment can turn into disappointment, and then the disappointment can eventually turn into disillusionment. However, the disillusionment cannot really be resolved because what you are longing for—the perfect house, the perfect job, the perfect husband—simply does not exist.

A REALITY CHECK

There are so many magical moments in motherhood: when your child is first placed in your arms, when you watch your toddler marvel over holding a caterpillar for the first time, when your preschooler first writes her name, when your fourth-grader wins the spelling bee, when your special needs child overcomes an obstacle for the very first time, when your pre-adolescent says, "You're the best mom in the world!," when your teenager is respectful over at the neighbor's house, and when your young adult walks across the stage to graduate from high school or college. Those are beautiful moments in the motherhood memory bank.

There are other delightful times: watching your kids play in the snow, playing Uno as a family, laughing around the dinner table, playing together at the park, camping for the first time, and enjoying vacations you'll never forget. Sometimes spontaneous and sometimes planned, these joy-filled, memory-making moments keep us going.

However, you and I both know those moments are not the stuff that happens 24/7/365. Life is full of challenges, mundane responsibilities, and difficult relationships. On one of my recent blog posts, I asked my online friends to share a one-word description of how they were feeling that day. Here are some of the responses shared from moms all over the world:

Worried	Anxious	Thankful
Stressed	Grateful	Fearful
Tired	Joyful	Betrayed
Hopeful	Encouraged	Confused
Overwhelmed	Abandoned	Discouraged
Sad	Stretched	Lonely
Emotional	Angry	Excited
Exhausted	Happy	Drained
Scared	Busy	Vulnerable
Waiting	Not-good-enough	Broken
Blessed	Stuck	

Can you relate to any of those words? If so, which ones? Whatever you are feeling, it's obvious that you are not alone. The responses are telling: more than 90 percent of the answers expressed negative emotions. Life is hard sometimes! If you feel this way and think no one understands, I hope you're starting to realize that many other women *do* understand.

You are not the only mom who feels worthless sometimes.

You are not the only mom who yelled at your children today.

You are not the only mom who is trying to blend two families into one and finding it far more difficult than you thought.

You are not the only mom who has struggled with infertility.

You are not the only mom who has had trouble bonding with an adopted child.

You are not the only mom who wishes her husband would just hold her and listen to her.

You are not the only mom who isn't making enough money to make ends meet.

You are not the only mom who constantly battles a weight issue.

You are not the only mom who struggles with your faith and understanding God.

You are not the only mom who is critical of her husband.

You are not the only mom who has said something to a friend that you later regretted.

You are not the only mom who feels as if she has no friends.

You are not the only mom who is struggling in her marriage.

You are not the only mom who has dealt with depression.

You are not the only mom facing conflict in her marriage about sex or money.

You are not alone. You are among friends.

You are not the only mom who has a difficult child or a wayward teenager.

You are not the only mom who has discovered your husband is addicted to pornography.

You are not the only mom who has discovered your husband has been unfaithful.

You are not the only mom who can't seem to keep up with the laundry and the house.

You are not the only mom who carries the title of "single mom."

You are not the only mom who struggled with breastfeeding her baby.

You are not the only mom who sometimes wants to run away.

You are not alone. You are among friends who struggle with these same issues. Unfortunately, most of us just don't talk about these "inside" issues often enough. That's why we feel alone or feel as if we've failed.

We're going to change that starting today. We may be contaminated with the Perfection Infection, but it's not without an antidote. Turn the page to discover the freedom found in authenticity.

Note

1. Justin and Trisha Davis, "The Masks We Wear," refine us (blog), May 9, 2011, http://refineus.org.

CHAPTER 2

THE *Antidote*

*I*t all started with the announcement that Michelle Duggar, star of the TLC show *Nineteen Kids and Counting*, would be the keynote speaker for our upcoming Hearts at Home conferences. I had watched the show a time or two and was intrigued by this mom who, along with her husband, decided to let God determine how many kids they would have. While I did not share their conviction to avoid birth control, I felt no animosity toward them because of their choices. However, that wasn't the case for some women. Once our keynote choice was announced, the "nastygrams" started arriving.

Some came from women who struggled with infertility and took personal offense to the fact that the Duggars have "more than their fair share" of children. Others claimed there was no way this couple could responsibly parent nineteen children. Still others chided us for bringing in a "celebrity." Every one of those letter writers announced she would not be attending the upcoming events. That made me sad, but what made me even sadder was that each of those women (and in some cases "groups of women") missed an incredible learning opportunity and the camaraderie that comes from gathering with nearly 6,300 other moms who understand what the mothering life is like. More than a dozen other speakers presented nearly thirty different workshops, and there was a second keynote message by psychologist Dr. Julianna Slattery about seeking wisdom. The conference was a powerful experience, and some of the messages I heard that weekend are still challenging me personally.

It grieved me that some moms let harsh, critical judging keep them from a wonderful event that could have benefitted them personally. It made me sad that pride robbed someone of a wonderful opportunity to laugh, learn, and find the refreshment of a weekend designed just for her.

All of us struggle with issues that clutter our hearts and keep us comparing ourselves to others. These issues also keep us perpetuating the Perfection Infection rather than eradicating it from our lives. Pride, fear, insecurity, and judging perpetuate the Perfection Infection that taints our hearts and plagues our society. When those attitudes creep into our hearts, we miss out. We cheat ourselves out of a great experience, a new friendship, or a deeper conversation.

What does it take to start to recognize our heart issues? How can we remove the masks we both knowingly and unknowingly hide behind to find the experience of authenticity we long for? I've found the shift

....

to be rather like changing clothes. You take off one garment and put on another. The Bible says it this way: "You were taught . . . to **put off** your old self, which is being corrupted by its deceitful desires . . . and to **put on** the new self, created to be like God in true righteousness and holiness" (Ephesians 4:22–24, emphasis mine).

Pride sneaks in, and sometimes we mistake it for confidence.

TAKE OFF PRIDE AND PUT ON HUMILITY

Pride sneaks in, and sometimes we mistake it for confidence. However, pride is comparing ourselves, knowingly or unknowingly, to others with the result that we come out looking better than they do.

Pride is a thief. It robs us of our joy because we become obsessed with believing we deserve something better than what we have. It cheats us of God's plan for our lives because we demand our own way. Pride robs us of knowledge because we already know it all. It keeps us from experiencing healing because we refuse to forgive, and we wouldn't dream of admitting we are wrong. It steals intimacy from our relationship with God because "I can do it myself." Pride damages relationships because "I'm right and you're wrong." It keeps us from deep friendships because we are unwilling to be honest and transparent.

Pride is cleverly costumed in our lives. On the outside it looks like confidence. Inside, it operates as false security.

Entitlement is a side-effect of pride. If you've ever uttered the words, "That's not fair," or "I deserve better," or "I should have been given . . ." you've harbored pride in your heart.

Pride is self-centered, self-focused, self-preserving. It's all about *I* and *me*. For instance, pride can creep into our marriages when "I do" becomes "I do it better than you." Pride keeps us from apologizing when we're wrong. Pride builds walls, crushes kindness, and kills intimacy.

Pride raises its ugly self in our relationships with other moms. In order to feel better about ourselves, we try to find ways that we are "better" than another. Most of the time these comparisons stay in our heads, but they consistently put distance between us and another person.

Shouldn't we be able to feel confident without that confidence being prideful? Absolutely. There is a difference between pride and self-confidence. Pride demands a voice. Self-confidence is quiet, undemanding, and unassuming. Pride believes you are better. Self-confidence believes you are capable. Pride is about taking. Self-confidence is about offering.

So how do pride or self-confidence play out in my daily life as a mom? Pride demands that situations be handled *my* way at my moms group. Self-confidence respects the leaders and guidelines established for the group, and it doesn't take difficult situations personally. Pride sees only how *my* child was wronged in a situation. Self-confidence realizes that my child could have been just as wrong as another child or could have contributed to a difficult situation at school. Pride demands that *I* be lauded for my efforts as a volunteer or employee. Self-confidence performs the job confidently without expecting a pat on the back.

More than anything, pride wraps a tight chain around our hearts, keeping us bound up with anger, demands, and unforgiveness. It poisons and robs us of the joys of life. It also perpetuates our drive for perfection, which ultimately sets us up for failure.

·········

So if I "take off" pride, what do I "put on" in its place? The answer is humility.

If you are a member of the human race, you probably struggle with this one. We live in a "Me, me, me," society. Humility says, "You, you, you." We moms tend to put others first when the others are our kids, but we don't necessarily do it as well in other relationships. Our human nature wants to do what we want to do. "If I don't push for my own way, people will walk all over me," we might think privately.

While humility feels weak, the truth is that humility is a sign of great strength. Humility is about putting ego aside. The word *humility* comes from a Latin word *humilitas*, which means grounded or low. When we are "grounded," we aren't easily swayed. We stand firm in who we are, who we belong to, and who we are committed to be going forward. A grounded person isn't looking for recognition because she is at peace with her worth in God's eyes.

Humility is also about submission. A humble person submits to authority. *Submission* is not a word that many of us embrace. However, before you throw this book across the room, consider the concept of submitting a little further. When we allow God to lead our lives, we submit to His leadership. We do this because we trust Him as our Creator and we believe He has our best interests in mind. The more we are able to submit, the more peace we experience. God tells us in the Bible, "Do nothing out of selfish ambition or vain conceit. Rather, in humility, value others above yourselves, not looking to your own interests but each of you to the interests of the others" (Philippians 2:3).

Most of the time pride and humility play a tug-of-war inside of us. Pride believes "I can do it myself," and humility says, "I can't do this without you, God." So what does this have to do with the Perfection Infection and motherhood?

Our longing to handle life "perfectly" keeps us bound up trying. We're trying to be the best mom we can be. We're trying to put on a good game face so others will believe we're doing better than we actually are. We're trying to convince ourselves that if we just work a little harder, we'll become the moms we think we should be. In all that trying, we're really being dishonest with others and even more so with ourselves.

God sees us through eyes of grace. It is as if He is saying, "Don't keep striving so that you can feel good about your accomplishments. Instead, live in My grace. Yes, do motherhood well—even with excellence. But know that I love you just as you are—no 'perfection' necessary. Come find freedom in an authentic relationship with Me and with others."

Your honesty will be a catalyst for someone else's honesty.

In the book of Proverbs, we read, "When pride comes, then comes disgrace, but with humility comes wisdom" (Proverbs 11:2). Wow! Humility brings wisdom. I know I need more of that! Here's more: "Pride leads to conflict; those who take advice are wise" (Proverbs 13:10 NLT). Humility says, "I still have a lot to learn, so I'll gladly take advice from others."

Take off the mask of pride today. You'll be doing yourself and the moms in your mothering community a huge favor. When pride is removed, honesty happens. Then you will discover that your honesty will be a catalyst for someone else's honesty and change might also take place in other moms' lives.

· · · · · · · ·

TAKE OFF FEAR AND PUT ON COURAGE

My finger hovered over the button on my computer mouse. One click, and the world would know. One click, and my broken world would become public knowledge.

Three days earlier my husband had walked out of our marriage. While he'd been struggling with disillusionment with life for months, I never thought he'd walk away from all he had once loved.

Living in the public eye, I had two choices: put on my game face and pretend all is well, or be honest about my broken world and broken heart. I opted for honesty, but the fear was almost paralyzing as I prepared to share my heart with a candid blog post.

What would people think? How would I be judged? What nasty emails and blog comments would I have to deal with?

I'm an honest author and speaker. My books and messages are usually built equally around my successes and failures. I don't do *fake*. Even though I'm used to being vulnerable in public, this exposure felt like nakedness on a new level. I could taste the bitter fear as I swallowed the reality of my new circumstances.

I summoned all the courage I could find and clicked "publish" on my blog dashboard. Then I went upstairs, curled into a ball in my bed, and cried myself to sleep. The pain was so intense. My heart literally hurt. I could hear my friend Crystal talking with my two teenagers in the kitchen downstairs. *Thank you, God, for my friends, who are loving me and taking care of my family in the midst of my oh-so-imperfect life.*

I napped fitfully for a couple of hours. When I awoke, I remembered the words I had put out to the world before I crawled into my bed. Fear found its way into my head again. What would people think?

. . . .

I made my way downstairs slowly, stopping to talk to both of my brokenhearted teenage sons along the way. They had shed more tears in the past three days than at any other time in their lives, but they seemed to be weathering this crisis better than I was at that moment.

Without thinking, I made my way to the computer, clicked on the recent post, and saw dozens of comments had been posted. I braced myself for the criticism, but instead I saw love, hope, and encouragement. Words of truth offset the lies that were fueling the fear. Words of empathy, grace, and mercy reached out from the computer screen to give me a much-needed cyber hug.

I had prepared myself for some of the same kind of feedback we'd received with the Michelle Duggar announcement, but I saw none of it that day—and very little in the days and weeks to come. Yes, there was some negative pushback, but not nearly what I feared I might have to endure.

Much of the time fear keeps us from being honest with other moms. We fear what others will think. We fear appearing weak or less than perfect. We fear that we'll be "found out"—that others will realize we don't have it as together on the inside as we portray on the outside. We fear the judgment and criticism of others. We fear rejection.

Truthfully, some of that fear is valid. Sometimes judgment and criticism happen. However, most of the time, they don't. In the meantime, though, our fears have taken on a life of their own, keeping us from the honest relationships we crave. Fear breeds isolation because we are just sure no one else has *ever* felt this way before. We are sure we're the *only* one facing this crisis.

Someone once described fear as **F**alse **E**vidence **A**ppearing **R**eal.

. . . .

A Swedish proverb states, "Worry gives a small thing a big shadow." Both aphorisms are so true. We convince ourselves that something is bigger than it really is. We "awfulize" it in our mind. However, much of the time what we worry about—or fear—never comes into reality. We waste our time and energy on this thief that perpetuates the Perfection Infection and keeps us isolated from others.

So if we are to "take off" fear, what do we replace it with? We have to "put on" courage. It was Eleanor Roosevelt who said, "You gain strength, courage, and confidence by every experience in which you really stop to look fear in the face, . . . You must do the thing you think you cannot do." Doing the thing you think you cannot do is courage! Courage is not the absence of fear. Instead, it is the determination that something else is more important than the fear.

Courageous women are still fearful; they just don't allow fear to stop them. If we're waiting for the fear to go away so the courage can take its place, it will never happen. Instead, courage appears on the scene while fear is still very present.

In the Bible, God says, "Be strong and courageous. Do not be afraid; do not be discouraged, for the Lord your God will be with you wherever you go" (Joshua 1:9). Our courage comes from knowing we are not alone. God is with us. He is our strength. He will help us take off fear and put on courage.

So who do we need to be honest with? First, ourselves. If we internally expect perfection, we will constantly be dissatisfied, disappointed, and discouraged. We need the courage to be honest with ourselves that perfection is impossible. We need to cut ourselves some slack, see ourselves through eyes of grace, love ourselves—with our imperfections included.

....

The best way to do this is to see ourselves through God's eyes. He loves us, flaws and all. He sees us through eyes of grace. The more we understand His unconditional love for us, the more we can learn to love ourselves and others unconditionally. We need to let God define us. If we do that, we can rest in our imperfection, knowing His love is not based on our behavior. This is one of the best antidotes we can administer to ourselves in the battle against the poisonous Perfection Infection.

Once we're honest with ourselves, it's much easier to be honest with others. If our true value is based on how God sees us, then it is easier for us to be honest with others, because what they think about us or how they respond no longer defines us. Honesty begets honesty. Your honesty will help draw out the honesty of others. By admitting your needs, you create a safety zone for your friends to do the same.

My decision to be honest about my hurting marriage was a hard one to make. Yet by taking off fear and putting on courage, God opened the floodgates. The emails and Facebook messages poured in from other women who were also facing difficult marriage issues. I didn't expect that! God was allowing my pain to help others who were also in pain. I didn't necessarily have answers for them. Instead, I had empathy and compassion. When you're in pain, one of the most important things to do is connect with others who understand what your life is like. I discovered that my honesty allowed others to be honest, too. We all took off our masks and got honest. No perfection—just real life that is sometimes hard. My husband is now back home, and God is doing His best work to make good out of something the enemy meant for evil. I am very grateful.

....

The Perfection Infection gains ground when fear prevails. It loses its control over us when courage succeeds. Take off fear and put on courage today. It will help you stand firm in who you are and will keep you less influenced by others.

TAKE OFF INSECURITY AND PUT ON CONFIDENCE

"I'm afraid I'll break him," said Tonya as the nurse placed her newborn son into her tentative arms.

"Don't worry, Tonya," the nurse replied. "You are everything your son needs."

Some of us come into motherhood feeling confident in our abilities. We babysat when we were in junior high and high school. Some of us had younger siblings we helped care for. Others are just natural nurturers who transition into motherhood without a hitch.

Many moms, however, struggle with feeling competent for the job. We doubt our abilities. We question if we really have what it takes to raise this child. We reel when we mess up. We condemn ourselves when we lose our patience.

Insecurity happens when the voices inside our heads tell us we aren't enough. *I'm not patient enough to be a good mom. I'm not experienced enough to be President of the PTO. I'm not educated enough to be a good homeschooling mom. I'm not brave enough to quit my job and find another. I'm no good at friendships. I'm not smart enough to learn to do that on the computer.*

"*I can't*" *is more believable than* "*I can.*"

The negative voices that play in our heads keep us feeling "less than" others. Not only that, but they paralyze us from living out our full potential. "I can't" is more believable than "I can."

When we are battling the Perfection Infection, insecurity paralyzes us in so many ways. If I want to conquer the clutter in my house, but I want perfection (i.e., I want my house to look like a magazine!), I will likely not even start the job because deep down I know I can't do it perfectly. Perfectionism is the best friend to procrastination. I love how Marla Cilley, known online as "The FlyLady," puts it. She says, "A good enough job done today is better than the perfect job *not* done tomorrow." So true!

Insecurity is also a cousin to fear. When we need to step out in courage, insecurity keeps the "what if's" in front of us. *What if I say the wrong thing? What if I say I can do this, but then I find out I really can't? What if I let her down? What if . . . ?* Sometimes we can "what if?" ourselves right into the fetal position!

If insecurity keeps us locked up in doubts, confidence is the key that will unlock the insecurity chains that bind us. Insecurity says, "I can't." Confidence says, "I can because God will show me how!"

True confidence is really "God-confidence." It's not so much about believing in ourselves as it is about believing in what God can do through us. It's changing the message inside our heads from "I can't" to "God can!" The Bible confirms this in Jeremiah 17:7: "But blessed are those who trust in the Lord and have made the Lord their hope and confidence" (NLT).

Confidence recognizes a divine design. You and I are created to do life in relationship with the God who created us. His grace covers over our imperfections. When we learn to see ourselves through God's eyes, we can embrace our imperfections and rest in His love and grace.

Confidence also happens when we celebrate who God made us to be, rather than lament who we aren't. Insecurity keeps us looking at other women, longing to be who they are: more creative, skinnier, smarter, more patient, a better cook. The list goes on and on. However, confidence happens when we embrace our strengths and our weaknesses. We see them as a fingerprint of who we are designed to be. We find contentment in being who we are, not who we aren't.

What would this look like in a practical way? Let's say you're doing a little Internet surfing and you pop over to Pinterest. If you use Pinterest only to gather ideas and keep them organized for easy retrieval, it can be a helpful little website. However, too many of us move from idea gathering to playing that nasty old comparison game. We see so many wonderful ideas and how other women do things and we begin thinking, *I'm a terrible mom because I don't make my children's food look like a picture.* Or, *I'm failing because my home is not organized the way it should be.* Insecurity says, *Oh no, I'm not measuring up. I'm not as good a mom as this person is.* Confidence says, *Good for these ladies who share their ideas. I'm glad we're not all made from the same mold. Those are great ideas, but many of them are not for me. I'm not crafty or artsy, but I'm comfortable in my own unique skin.*

If you want to rid yourself of the Perfection Infection, begin to move from insecurity to confidence. Take your eyes off yourself and put them on God. He will equip you with whatever you need for the relationships and responsibilities given to you. Insecurity is bondage to who we're not. Confidence is freedom in who we are!

....

TAKE OFF JUDGMENT AND PUT ON GRACE

Emily pulled into the parking lot at the local park. As soon as she parked, her girls bounded out of the car and headed toward their favorite playground equipment. Emily followed close behind. She loved taking her girls to the park.

As Emily and the girls laughed and played, Emily noticed a couple of children at the park who didn't have a parent playing with them. Then she noticed her: a mom sitting in her car. It soon became obvious these children playing alone belonged to this "irresponsible" mom. *Can't you get out of the car?* Emily thought. *Is it asking too much of you to play with your kids?*

While most of us hesitate to admit it, we've all had those thoughts about another mom. Maybe it's someone we know or maybe it's a complete stranger we walk by at the park, grocery store, or school parking lot. Our judgmental spirit kicks in without us even realizing it.

Fast-forward six months. Emily is now pregnant with child number three, and this pregnancy is a difficult one. The nausea is out of control, and she can barely function. One afternoon her girls beg her to play at the park. Emily initially resists their pleas but finally agrees to drive them there. "Girls, I'll take you to the park, but Mommy can't play with you today. I'm just so sick."

As they drove to park, the nausea increased. When they pulled into the parking lot, Emily found a parking spot near the playground equipment so she could keep an eye on her girls. As she sat in the car, willing herself not to vomit, she became increasingly sickened by another thought. *Oh my goodness. Now I'm "that mom," the one who can't get out of her car to play with her kids. If any other mom pulls into this parking lot she will think the worst of me like I did about that other mom so many months ago!*

What Emily experienced is called conviction. God used this situation to convict her of judging that mother so many months ago. Conviction is a good thing because it holds us accountable and motivates us to change. Emily realized the unfair judgment she had made about the other mom and was now, more than ever, aware of the dangers of judging.

I'm proud of Emily. I'm proud of the way she examined her heart and allowed that gentle correction from God. I'm proud of her for having the courage to share this story with her mom, who eventually shared it with me. However, I don't think Emily is alone in her tendency to judge. If we're honest, I think most of us will acknowledge that we more often see one another through eyes of criticism rather than of grace.

Emily could have pulled into that parking lot the first time and had compassion on that mom. She could have thought, *I wonder why she's not playing with her kids. Maybe she's nurturing a broken heart or grieving the loss of a parent or even a child. Maybe her marriage is a mess, and she just can't pull herself together. Maybe she's ill, struggling with something terrible like cancer or another debilitating illness. Maybe she's just horribly sick from an otherwise healthy pregnancy.*

If I'm completely honest with myself, I will admit I would probably have done exactly what Emily did the first time. That breaks my heart, but it's true. I don't want to be that way! Why is it that we tend to think the worst of other moms? What keeps us from giving one another the benefit of the doubt? Why do we jump to judgment instead of giving one another grace?

....

This is where the Perfection Infection has become an epidemic. It no longer infects just us with pride, fear, and insecurity. Now we impose our "perfect" expectations on others: our kids, our spouses, our friends, and even complete strangers. This is the sickness that started "The Mommy Wars," pitting stay-at-home moms against working moms. Judging has built walls between us, and it's time to tear down those walls.

Judging is ugly. It demands. It criticizes. It divides. It destroys. It blinds us to our own faults. Judging imposes our opinions on other people. It leaves little room for others to be different from us because it sees those differences as wrong.

If you peel away the layers of judging you'll find pride at its core. Pride says, "I know best," or "My way is the best way," or "You don't know how to do this as well as I do." For many of us, a critical spirit of judgment is very present in our marriages. The man who could do no wrong before we had children, can do no right now that we have children. He can't diaper them right, can't bathe them right, can't dress them right, and certainly can't care for them well in my absence.

Sometimes judging creeps into our parenting. As children get older, they have their own opinions. They begin to make their own decisions. Their personalities emerge, and if they are in any way different from us (or worse yet, challenging in the same ways we are), we can become critical without much thought to the damage we are inflicting.

When we spend time with a friend and her kid's misbehavior begins to grate on our nerves, judging can creep in. We think thoughts like, *If she would only answer him the first time, he wouldn't have to say "Mommy" twenty times!* or *She's not consistent enough with her discipline. If she would just be more consistent, she'd have better-behaved kids.* Without realizing it, we've begun to build a wall. Judging is the brick, and pride is the mortar holding the judging attitudes in place.

Grace is when we deserve punishment but we get mercy instead.

This strain of the Perfection Infection is so dangerous that it calls for a strong antidote. We need God's strength and wisdom and, more than anything else, His example to help us heal from this controlling disease.

The cure for judgment is grace. And just what is grace? Grace is when we deserve punishment but we get mercy instead. Grace is at the core of our relationship with God. God's grace doesn't have to be earned. Instead, it is freely given. We just have to accept it. What a beautiful gift!

In human relationships, grace is allowing others to be human, to make mistakes and not get criticized for every little thing they do wrong or differently from the way we do it. Sometimes you and I waste so much time and energy nitpicking the littlest things that our spouses, our children, our friends, and our neighbors do. We jump to conclusions about people we do not know. What would our lives look like if we replaced judging with grace? What freedom would we experience if we became grace-givers instead of judgment-makers?

Let's start with ourselves. Sometimes we're hard on others because we're so hard on ourselves. Since our expectations are off the charts, we are constantly disappointed with ourselves and others. What would happen if you said this to yourself the next time you make a mistake: "I'm not perfect and that was a screwup. We all make mistakes, so I'm going to give myself grace, learn from my mistake, make any necessary apologies, and move on." That's it. No beating yourself up, no replaying the incident over and over in your mind, no voice inside your head calling you names. Can you imagine the freedom we could experience if we let go of our expectations about not making mistakes?

Let's think about how being a grace-filled woman might affect a marriage. My friend Carolyn let grace come into her marriage. One day after being "corrected" for the umpteenth time about how he filled the dishwasher, her husband, John, threw up his hands and said, "I can't do anything right in your eyes!" At first, Carolyn backpedaled and tried to rationalize why she thought her way was better. But then she stopped herself and realized that John was right. She criticized every little thing he did because—if she was honest with herself—she thought her way was better. Oh, the damage we do with a critical spirit! From that conversation forward, Carolyn committed to replace criticism with grace. She found it meant that she had to keep her mouth shut far more often than she was accustomed to! But in time, their marriage began to experience a healing from a sickness she hadn't even known was there.

What would it look like to give grace more often to our kids? Would it mean we were "too soft" in our parenting? Would it lower our expectations and diminish their sense of responsibility? Actually, grace would do the opposite. First, we would compliment them more often than criticizing them. This doesn't give children big heads. Instead it gives them big hearts. A child who grows up in a critical environment easily becomes a critical person. If a child feels supported, loved, and valued, that child can grow into a kind, sensitive, loving adult. Second, children living in a grace-filled family understand that it is okay to fail.

. . . .

They learn, in fact, that making mistakes is a part of life. We learn from our mistakes. We grow stronger. We move through life better. We realize that failing is a natural part of the human experience. A grace-filled parent sets the pace for this life-giving home environment.

Outside of family relationships, replacing judgment with grace can turn the world into a kinder, gentler place to live. It will turn churches into safe places for relationships to be nurtured. It will make moms groups enjoyable places to find friendships. It will make taking our kids to the park when we're sick and choosing to sit in the car an okay thing to do on occasion because people would view us through eyes of compassion. Wow! Can you imagine the freedom grace could bring to our lives and the healing it would bring to our relationships?

Our world needs more compassion, more mercy, and definitely more grace. Let's commit to make that change today. You and I can make a difference in this world, one grace-filled response at a time.

WATCH THOSE EXPECTATIONS

Jamie attended a Hearts at Home conference for the first time and wrote a blog post afterward reflecting on her time spent with other moms. She realized she is in desperate need to "control her crazy." She's realizing she has to do something about her skewed expectations.

> I am definitely a mom who feels crazy on a daily basis. Crazy for scheduling pictures with a live rabbit for Easter. Crazy because of all of the plates I'm trying to juggle. Crazy because I feel like I *should* have a healthy, warm, hearty dinner on the table and instead my kids are eating peanut butter and jelly—again. And while it doesn't make my crazy go away, it definitely helps me to

....

control my crazy when I realize that almost all of the moms I know are feeling the exact same way.

The consensus I came to with my friends as we were talking is that our crazy really all boils down to skewed expectations. In our minds, we have created certain ideals — those "shoulds" of life, so to speak — and when those expectations aren't met, my crazy spirals. When I place a peanut butter and jelly sandwich on the table, a small part of me feels like I'm failing — because I'm not meeting the (exceedingly high) expectations I have for myself as a mother. I feel guilty. I feel like a bad mother. And that's just a very minuscule example. When it comes to the big picture ideals I've set, my feelings and negative self-talk are much worse.[1]

Jamie has hit the nail on the head when she talks about skewed expectations. Our expectations are often what keep us from enjoying our real lives, our real families, our real bodies, and our real houses. Most of the time our expectations are unrealistic and incongruent with the realities of life. However, I don't believe we need to *lower* our expectations. I believe we need to *change* our expectations. *Lowering expectations* seems to indicate that we're "settling" for something less. *Changing expectations* indicates a need to transform or modify our thinking. More often than not, we need to change our perspective to better cope with real life. We need to change unrealistic expectations to realistic expectations.

When we shift our hopes and desires to the realm of reality, we'll be less often disappointed in ourselves and others. We'll embrace imperfection and the freedom of authenticity. In the coming pages, you'll hear the call to change expectations in addition to applying the

. . . .

Perfection Infection antidotes. As we move from idealism to realism, we will actually experience that sense of contentment, honesty, and peace we all long for.

We've explored how we unfairly compare ourselves to others, established that we all struggle with the same challenges in life one way or another, and identified how our culture has been inundated with the Perfection Infection by the media and technology.

We've also identified what keeps the Perfection Infection wreaking havoc on our lives and the antidotes that can begin to eradicate this awful disease that affects the way we view ourselves and others. We've also established that unrealistic expectations keep us feeling frustrated and discontent. Now it's time for us to apply this new knowledge to specific areas of our lives. Perfect bodies, perfect marriages, perfect kids, and perfect houses just don't exist. So how do we change our expectations and make peace with the imperfect parts of life, finding the authenticity we're really longing for?

Turn the page to discover what "real life" looks like when moms take off their masks, get honest, and reveal their imperfect selves. You'll find that your "imperfect" life is not so different from the imperfect lives of other moms. You're not nearly as alone as you sometimes feel that you are. Most importantly though, there is incredible freedom to be found when we can really embrace that reality.

Note

1. Jamie Weitl, "Control Your Crazy," Liberating Working Moms (blog), March 30, 2012, http://liberatingworkingmoms.com.

CHAPTER 3

NO MORE *Perfect* KIDS

*O*ne of my teenagers had a friend spend the night, and the two boys asked if they could sleep in the basement rec room. Since they had slept down there many times before, I allowed them to watch a late movie and sleep downstairs.

At three o'clock in the morning, these two teenage boys walked into my bedroom and woke me from a deep sleep.

"Mom," said the one who belongs to me. "Um . . . Mom . . . we kind of snuck out of the house."

"What?" I mumbled, barely awake.

"Mom . . . well . . . we kind of decided to sneak out of the house and go get some McDonald's . . . and um . . . well . . . we kind of got pulled over by a police officer because we had a taillight out on the car . . .

. . . .

and . . . um . . . we kind of got in trouble for curfew . . . and well . . . the police officer is kind of downstairs in the kitchen and he kind of wants to talk to you."

"What are you 'kind of' talking about?" I responded, willing myself to wake up. "This isn't a funny joke, guys."

Kids make mistakes. Welcome to motherhood.

I heard nervous laughter from both boys. "We wish it was a joke, but it's not. Can you come talk to the police officer who's downstairs?"

I stumbled out of bed, threw on my bathrobe, and made it down the stairs to the kitchen. Indeed, there *was* a police officer in my house at 3 a.m.

Such a beautiful reminder: There are no perfect kids.

Now if you're a mom of a two-year-old, that story just might freak you out a bit. Don't let it. Instead, let it provide a reality check. Kids make mistakes. They make poor choices sometimes—whether they are two years old and decide to throw a fit in the grocery store or they are seventeen and decide to sneak out of the house. That's real life. Welcome to motherhood.

With five children, my husband and I have dealt with our fair share of "real kid" challenges: misbehaving in public, lying, cheating, stealing, skipping school. We've had to manage ADHD and the learning challenges of an internationally adopted child who didn't speak English until the age of nine. There have been big issues, too, like experimenting with alcohol and cigarettes, making poor relationship choices, and rebelling against church and faith.

If you're a mom of little ones, just reading this may be making you fret about the future. If you are a mom of teenagers, you are likely

. . . .

breathing a sigh of relief knowing you are not the only one. Regardless of what season of motherhood you are in, let's share the reality check: *Your kids are not perfect.* Their imperfections are not a reflection of you. You can't "control" them into perfection. Allowing your children to fail—without getting your anger as a consequence—is a gift to them. The most beautiful thing you can offer them is your imperfect self who does her best to handle their imperfections with love and grace.

WATCH THOSE EXPECTATIONS

Parents need to cast vision for their children. We need to set standards for achievement and behavior as well as offer boundaries to help point each child to those standards and goals. Whether its potty-training a toddler or defining boundaries for a teenager, setting expectations is an important part of parenting.

But expectations are misplaced when we, as parents, expect ourselves to be perfect and expect our kids to be perfect. With those expectations, we will always end up disappointed and disillusioned. We need to adjust our expectations to anticipate mistakes and even foresee misbehavior. Sounds kind of pessimistic, doesn't it? Or is it simply realistic?

Unrealistic expectations keep us perpetually disappointed—in ourselves and in our kids. That's not a healthy way to live. It's not healthy for us personally and it does not contribute to a healthy family environment for any child.

Many times, we don't even realize we are expecting our kids to be perfect. If someone would ask us if we expect perfection, we would defensively respond, "Absolutely not!" However, sometimes our expectations are unconscious ones. We know, rationally, that no one is perfect, so we claim not to expect perfection. However, in reality, we are frustrated every time we have to deal with behavior issues. If we really got honest with ourselves, we would have to admit that we really do expect perfection or at least something close to it.

See if this little quiz can help you get honest with yourself.

✲ True or False? ✲

✦ I am very pleased with who my child is, and I wouldn't change one thing about his or her personality or giftedness.

✦ When I make a mistake, I forgive myself and move on. I rarely think about it again.

✦ I am (or I will be) perfectly okay with my child not getting mostly A's on a report card.

✦ It doesn't embarrass me when my child fails; I help, if I can, and then move on. We try not to bring up the mistakes of the past.

✦ I want to help my child succeed in his/her life goals and relationships, but I don't make too many plans, since my child will make his/her own choices.

✦ I honestly evaluate my child's God-given abilities, instead of having him/her participate in activities I like (or liked as a kid).

✦ I appreciate the ways my child is different from me.

✦ When I do something foolish, I am able to laugh at myself.

✦ When my child does something foolish, we are able to laugh about it together.

✦ I rarely respond with anger if my child makes a mess.

If you answered false to five or more of these questions, you probably have high expectations of yourself and your child. The first step to setting realistic expectations is to recognize the unrealistic expectations you currently have. Unrealistic expectations discourage. Realistic expectations inspire. Cut yourself some slack, give your child some grace, and watch the dynamics in your family change before your very eyes!

Does the Mommy Monster show up at your house on occasion? When the Mommy Monster yells, her anger affects the whole family. Several years ago I began to realize she was showing up at my house more often than I was comfortable with. When I examined what dynamics brought the appearance of the Mommy Monster, I realized that my unrealistic expectations were contributing to my craziness. I was not accurately estimating my children's actual abilities. Bottom line: I was expecting too much too soon.

I recently noticed a young mom struggling with this same problem of expecting too much too soon. She was frustrated with her two-year-old constantly pushing the limits. She was also trying to potty-train the two-year-old. She wanted the boundary battles to stop, and she wanted her daughter out of diapers. The problem is that neither of those goals was possible for her two-year-old to reach, especially while tackling them at the same time. This well-intentioned mom was not accurately estimating her child's actual abilities. She was expecting too much too soon, which resulted in added stress for herself and her child.

Many of us overestimate our children's ability to exercise self-control, to stay focused on a task, and to handle social situations. It's normal for a two-year-old to get upset if he doesn't get something he wants. It's normal for a three-year-old to lose it if there's a change in his bedtime

· · · · · · · ·

routine. It's normal for a five-year-old to daydream in the middle of a T-ball game. It's normal for a twelve-year-old to be moody. It's normal for a teenager to be irresponsible every once in a while.

Too often, we let our own impatience take the lead and we scold with an angry voice because deep down we expect them to act better than they are. We lose perspective of what is normal behavior for their age and stage of development. We get angry because they don't live up to our off-the-charts expectations, and then the Mommy Monster shows up full force. This happens all the way from the toddler years through the teen years and even into the young adult years.

In my book *Got Teens?* coauthored with Pam Farrel, we talked about this very issue with teenagers:

> Dr. Jay Giedd, at the National Institute of Health, has been conducting a thirteen-year study into the mind of teens. He and his colleagues at UCLA, Harvard, and Montreal Neurological Institute have discovered some interesting insights. It used to be believed that a child's brain was nearly complete by age twelve, but Dr. Giedd has discovered what all of us moms of teens have known all along—they aren't all grown up yet! (He might have also experienced this at home—he has four teens, too!) The good doctor found that the brain undergoes dramatic changes well past puberty. The medical community is looking at how brain development might impact those traits we as moms are so aware of: emotional outbursts, reckless risk taking, rule breaking, and toying with things like sex, drugs, and rock and roll . . .
>
> The brain seems to develop from back to front. The functions that mature earliest are in the back of the brain, like those that

. . . .

control interaction with the environment: vision, hearing, touch, spatial processing, etc. Next to develop are areas that help you coordinate those interactions, for example the part of the brain that helps you find the bathroom light switch in the dark because you know it's there even when you can't see it. The very last part of the brain to be pruned and shaped to its adult dimensions is the prefrontal cortex, home of the so called executive functions — planning, setting priorities, organizing thoughts, suppressing impulses, weighing the consequences of one's actions. In other words, the final part of the brain to grow up is the part capable of deciding, *I'll finish my homework, and take out the garbage, and then I'll text my friends about seeing a movie.*

So when is a teen mature? They can vote and serve in the military at eighteen, they are allowed to drink and gamble at twenty-one, but they can't rent a car till age twenty-five. The car companies might be the closest at guesstimating. Dr. Giedd sets maturity of the brain at around age twenty-five. Giedd says, "There is a debate over how much conscious control kids have. You can tell them to shape up or ship out, but making mistakes is part of how the brain optimally grows."[1]

There's some perspective for you. We expect maturity from our kids before they have the brain development to be fully mature! We need to make sure our expectations are realistic for their developmental stages of life.

There's a fine line here for us. We do need to expect responsibility. We do need to expect obedience. We do need to expect social skills after we teach and train them to those standards. But we also need to

....

expect them to fail at those things. Yep, you read that right. We need to expect them to fail; perfection doesn't exist. Not only that, we have to remember that making mistakes is actually part of how the brain grows. Mistakes are launching grounds for further learning. So handling their mistakes, their misbehavior, and their poor choices is part of our job as a parent. If we expect perfection, then we are actually getting in the way of the natural maturing process—which is what we want to happen in the first place!

Why do we find it so difficult to let our children make mistakes? I believe there are several reasons:

1) *We want control.* It's hard to let go and let our kids take responsibility, make mistakes, and have control of some aspects of their life.

2) *We want to be needed.* We want to be involved in our children's lives. It makes us feel good to help them succeed. If we're honest with ourselves, it's hard to just sit back and watch them struggle with something. We want to jump in and help.

3) *We want the approval of others.* Whether we like it or not, most of us play the comparison game with our kids. If my child's performance doesn't measure up at the piano recital, what are other parents going to think of me as a parent?

4) *We are fearful.* We're afraid they'll be emotionally scarred. We're afraid they'll resent us for not helping them or letting them fail.

5) *We are impatient.* Let's face it; allowing kids to figure things out is a slow process. We're all tempted to just do it for them because it makes life easier. Allowing a child to try, fail, try again, fail again, and try once more is tedious. There's no shortcut to learning; they have to do it themselves.

....

For some of us, the biggest reason it's so difficult for us to let our children make mistakes is that we can't stand the thought of them being less than perfect. We jump into the picture to smooth their rough corners because we fear that anything less than perfect reflects poorly on us.

So how do we resist the urge to rescue our kids? How do we keep from interfering with the growth that happens from trying, failing, and trying again? Start by partnering with the natural maturing process. Cast vision, set goals, give large doses of encouragement, but don't make every misbehavior a mountain to be scaled. Chalk some behaviors up to immaturity, and allow them to disappear or develop on their own with time. You don't have to point out every wrong thing your children do, especially when they are naturally immature. When you punish according to unrealistic expectations you exasperate the child. The Bible tells us, "Do not exasperate your children; instead, bring them up in the training and instruction of the Lord" (Ephesians 6:4). Punishing your children because of your unrealistic expectations stresses them out and leads to other negative behaviors, like anger or temper tantrums in the early years and rebellion during the teen years.

You are the leading expert on your child.

Remember, you are the leading expert on your child. It's okay for you to encourage your child to do his or her best while keeping the balance of not having unreasonable expectations. Even a slight adjustment in your expectations can bring huge relief to a child who really wants to do his best, but is limited by his level of maturity.

IT'S NOT PERSONAL

Jamie had gone head to head with her preteen all afternoon. By dinnertime when I talked with her on the phone, she declared, "I swear she's out to get me. She knows just what buttons to push to put me over the edge."

We've all been there. We're sure our kid is out to get us. We're sure their main goal is to send us to the loony farm.

Let me reassure you: It's not personal. Well, actually it is very personal for them—they want what they want—but it's not personal to you. It's not about you. Don't take their behavior personally.

Every toddler, child, and teenager wants his own way. It's human nature. Children will push their boundaries because independence is their ultimate goal (and as parents, that should be our ultimate goal too). That is normal.

A child's desire to be independent isn't about you. Teenagers want to leave home because they are longing for freedom. They may make you feel that their real reason is to get away from you, but it's to get away from anything that looks restrictive or requires accountability. You represent boundaries, so they naturally desire to break away. But their desire to break away can feel like a personal rejection if you don't recognize where it's really coming from.

We have to be careful about taking our children's actions personally, because the minute we do, we become ineffective parents. That's right. The minute we take their misbehavior personally, three things happen:

1) *We lose control.* Our child is suddenly "leading" us, and this puts us in the follower position.

2) *We become angry.* We are now offended by the child's behavior and become defensive and distracted by controlling or dealing with our anger.

3) *We lose focus.* When we take their behavior personally, we make their misbehavior about us (embarrassing us, exhausting us, etc.) instead of it being about their poor choices.

One mom told a story on her blog about a time when she took her son to a playground to meet up with some new mom friends. As she was talking with the moms, her son decided to get creative. Here is the story in Kasey's own words:

> I turned around to see my son, pants at his ankles, creating a 45-degree arch with his pee. The worst part was hearing him yell: "Run through the sprinkler!" to the slack-jawed and horrified children staring at him.
>
> I think the mothers around me saw my anger rising. Turning on my heels I was ready to unleash all the discipline techniques I knew. That's when one of my new mom friends touched my arm and smiled at me. I was in SHOCK! How could she be smiling!?!
>
> In a kind, compassionate voice she looked into my eyes. "We've all been there. I know you'll take care of it, but don't let your embarrassment decide his punishment. It *is* kind of funny."[2]

Those are words of wisdom for all of us. We could also add, "Don't let your anger decide his punishment." When we're in the middle of parenting, our kids do anger us. They do embarrass us. However, we have to learn to keep our emotions in check when dealing out consequences.

. . . .

This new friend was telling Kasey, and all of us: Don't take your child's behavior personally. It's not about you. Don't make it about you. Your kids are imperfect. They will do many things you never thought you'd be dealing with. Keep your perspective. See the humor in the situation (if you can!), and, above all else, keep the focus on your child.

BE A "YES" MOM!

One summer when my two youngest boys were in grade school, they ran inside and said, "Mom, it's so hot outside! Can we see if it's hot enough to cook an egg on the sidewalk?" The practical side of me started to say no, but I caught myself. *Why can't they try it? Why is my first thought always no? Why can't I say yes? Is it "wasting" an egg, or simply using it for a different, but just as valuable, purpose?*

I finally said, "Sure. If you want to try it, go ahead! Just wash off the sidewalk when you're done." They got an egg from the refrigerator and ran out of the house to try their science experiment.

After twenty-seven years of mothering, I'm finally learning to be a "yes" mom more than a "no" mom. It hasn't been an easy transition, but it is an important one. For years my interactions with my kids looked more like this:

"No, you can't fingerpaint." (It will make too much of a mess.)

"No, you can't bake cookies today." (I just mopped the kitchen floor!)

"No, you can't have a friend over today." (I'd have to go pick up or drop off the child.)

"No, you can't play in the snow." (I'm not in the mood for wet boots, snowsuits, and soaked hats and gloves.)

Over time, however, I started paying attention to the nos and my reasoning behind them. It usually had something to do with my selfishness. *I* didn't want to deal with a mess. *I* didn't want to be bothered. *I* didn't want to have more work to do. That's not fun to admit, but it was true. My selfishness robbed my kids of some of the joy of just being kids!

One afternoon the children asked, "Can we blow bubbles in the house?" I initially said no because bubbles have always been an outside activity. But then I thought about my answer. *Why can't they blow bubbles in the house? We have no-spill bubble cups! Why do I always say no so quickly?* Finally, I said, "Yes, you can blow bubbles in the house. Have a blast."

And they did.

And that day, I started being more of a "yes" mom, than a "no" mom.

Why do we say no more often than we say yes? Three reasons tap into our "perfect mom" syndrome:

1) *We don't want the hassle.* Some of their requests inconvenience us. It's hard to admit this, but this is where our selfishness kicks in.

2) *We lack flexibility.* Most of us have an idea in our heads of how our day will go. When the children pipe up with a spontaneous request, it's hard for us to switch gears to fit their idea into our plans.

3) *We are protective.* Our children's natural instinct is to explore and pursue independence. Our natural instinct as parents is to protect. Sometimes those two instincts conflict. To be a "yes" mom, we have to balance our desire to protect and their need to explore.

. . . .

Motherhood has caused me to come face-to-face with my less-than-wonderful qualities. Sometimes my kids bring out the worst in me. However, God doesn't waste a thing. He uses my kids to bring me to Him. When I come face-to-face with my shortcomings, my weaknesses, and my sin, it's a reminder of my need for a God who wants me to be more like Him each and every day.

Examine how you interact with your kids. Where does your *yuck* show up? Is it selfishness? Impatience? A feeling of being overwhelmed? When your selfishness, impatience, or anger rises to the surface, tell God you're sorry, ask Him for His strength, and move forward with His help. After all, it's not just our kids who need to mature. We moms still have some "growing up" to do as well.

Want to tackle your idealism head-on? Need to be more flexible with your "perfect plans"? Work on being a "yes" mom more than a "no" mom. You'll stretch yourself and at the same time bless your kids.

BEWARE THE COMPARE

We live in a constantly improving society. We naturally want what we don't have. Millions of people opted for the iPhone 5, even though they had a perfectly working iPhone 4S. Perfectly good televisions are put on the curb because they've been replaced with the latest and greatest. We're always comparing what we have to what we do not have.

If we're not careful, we can do this with our children, too. Think for a moment. Have you ever compared your child to:

Your child's friends? Without realizing it we can compare our kids to their peers. Doing so can make ourselves feel better (our child excels when compared to their friends) or make ourselves feel like we're not measuring up (our child fails when compared to their friends).

Your child's siblings? We don't intend to do this, but often we struggle with how different our kids are. We label one as "difficult" and another as "easy."

The imaginary perfect child? Too often there is an "ideal" child we create in our minds. Our child never measures up to this perfect child.

Yourself? We can easily impose our strengths, our likes, our learning styles onto our unsuspecting children, who are emotionally and academically wired differently from how we are.

It's easy to compare, but, oh, so damaging to our uniquely created children! Psalm 139:13–14 says, "For you created my inmost being; you knit me together in my mother's womb. I praise you because I am fearfully and wonderfully made." God knit your child together perfectly! He knew exactly what He was doing. That strong will your child exercises may someday make him an incredibly effective leader. Her ability to argue may be the very strength she needs to be a good lawyer. His sensitivity may make him a perceptive father. The traits you loathe or long to change need to be managed but not wished away.

When we compare our kids to others, to ourselves, or to the "perfect child" in our minds, we are not embracing their distinctive qualities and allowing them to develop into the unique people God created them to be.

This can also happen with our dreams for our children. Our hopes for our children often come from comparisons. We want to offer them the same opportunities we had, or we want to offer them better opportunities than we had. We long for them to be as successful as their siblings, or their classmates, or as other parents' kids at church.

However, these hopes and dreams don't always match up with who your children really are, how they're wired, or where their interests lie. You may desire for your child to excel at sports, but he may be more interested in piano than punting. You might like your daughter to enjoy ballet as you did, but she may be more interested in photography than pointe shoes. You may want your child to have lessons that you never had, but he may be more interested in math than music.

Then there's college. College is not a one-size-fits-all dream for parents. Some young adults find that working a job for a couple of years before college is a good strategy. Others may choose to enter an internship program or learn a trade. Still others may choose to marry and start a family without finishing college. Our dreams may simply not be realities for them.

There is always the possibility our children will make choices that seem to dampen our dreams and permanently change their future into something that looks more like a nightmare—at least initially. My friend Lisa experienced that recently when her nineteen-year-old son became a father. His plans for college changed now that he needs to work full-time to support a family. Another friend of mine found her college-aged daughter moving back home after mismanaging her finances. Those certainly aren't the dreams these moms had for their kids.

Reality may be determined by the interests and talents of each child. It may be determined by our differing goals. It may be that their choices determine a new reality we never thought we'd face. What do we do when our dreams clash with reality? We adjust our expectations and love our children unconditionally. Let's explore what that kind of love looks like.

IT'S ALL ABOUT LOVE

Relationships are sometimes so complicated. Why? It's because we're dealing with imperfect people. And what do we naturally want to do with imperfect people? We want to change them! However, if we work to change another person, it's likely that we love ourselves more than we love that person. Ouch.

There are some verses in the Bible known as the "Love Chapter." These are often read at weddings and associated with marital love. However, these verses apply to all kinds of loving and apply very well to loving our imperfect children.

> Love is patient, love is kind. It does not envy, it does not boast, it is not proud. It does not dishonor others, it is not self-seeking, it is not easily angered, it keeps no record of wrongs. Love does not delight in evil but rejoices with the truth. It always protects, always trusts, always hopes, always perseveres (1 Corinthians 13:4–7).

Let's see what we can glean from the "love chapter" in 1 Corinthians.

Love is patient. Am I patient with my child who is so different from me?

Love is kind. Am I kind when it takes my child twice the amount of time to do something than I think it should?

Love does not envy. Do I wish my child were more like this mom's son or that mom's daughter?

Love does not boast. Am I quick to share what my child does well or to hide areas when the child doesn't seem to measure up?

Love is not proud. Am I hesitant to share how I'm *really* doing or how my child is *really* doing out of a fear of what people will think?

Love does not dishonor others. Do I ever dishonor my child, demanding that child be someone other than the unique person God has made him or her to be?

Love is not self-seeking. Am I ever selfish in my interactions with my child?

Love is not easily angered. How much energy do I waste being angry at my child?

Love keeps no record of wrongs. Do I have an ongoing list in my head about everything my child has done wrong?

Love does not delight in evil but rejoices in the truth. Do I keep my mind focused on God's truth about my child?

Love protects. Do I protect this unique human being God entrusted to me even when he challenges my authority?

. . . .

Love trusts. Do I trust that God has a bigger picture in mind for this child's life? Do I believe God knows what his or her future holds and I don't?

Love hopes. Do I hope and believe the best for this child, or do I dread what tomorrow might bring?

Love perseveres. Do I keep my mind on the future possibilities rather than focusing on the difficulties and challenges I'm dealing with today?

Whew! That's a tall order! Don't worry: You're not alone in finding these love parameters challenging. I certainly don't get all of these right. Only God loves perfectly. You and I are to evaluate honestly and go to work on the places where God wants to grow us up.

Love makes it safe to fail.

The more we learn to love unconditionally and the more we provide an emotionally safe and relationally secure environment for our kids, the more love makes it safe to fail. Love embraces challenges with a heart of learning. Love allows our kids to be themselves.

Love doesn't turn the other way and ignore issues. Loving parents do address the issues their children have. Love sets boundaries and provides accountability.

Unconditional love, however, allows for differences, embraces failure, and celebrates individuality. Love is the strength that allows us to adjust expectations. Love provides the perspective not to take their behavior personally. Love allows us to say yes when everything inside our logical minds wants to say no. Love gives us the grace to embrace reality instead of chasing comparison. Love is the language that needs to be spoken between imperfect mom and imperfect child.

APPLY THE ANTIDOTE

Motherhood stretches us. If we'll allow it, God will use our children to smooth our rough edges and strengthen our character. If you are looking to escape the Perfection Infection in your mothering, choose one or more of these practical strategies to apply the antidotes.

Reject Pride and Embrace Humility

Sometimes it feels as if it's our children's sole responsibility in life to humble us. (Especially on a bad mom day!) Most of us have to actively reject pride in some way, or it will creep into our thinking and take over our emotions.

The next time you are with a group of moms who are sharing stories, share your most embarrassing mothering moment. (You know which one I'm talking about: the one story you've sworn you'll never tell anyone!) Resist the prideful thought that the story will cause you to look bad.

Actively choose not to select "touch up" services on your child's school picture.

When your child makes a poor choice, thank God for this humbling moment. Thank Him for the reminder that your child isn't perfect and neither are you. Ask Him to work in your heart and your child's heart through this situation.

When your child makes a good choice, thank God. Liberally give Him the credit for working in your child's life.

Reject Insecurity and Embrace Confidence

Insecure moms are yanked around by their children's behavior. Confident moms are unmoved by their children's misbehavior. You can practically apply your understanding with confidence.

Resist the urge to control your child's behavior. When your child throws a temper tantrum, simply step over the child (Dr. Kevin Leman humorously says to resist the urge to step *on* the child) and continue with your activities. Be secure enough in your role as mom to let the child experience the consequence of not having an audience for the tantrum performance.

If your child misbehaves in a public setting, simply say to those who are witnessing the event, "This is something we're working on learning. Excuse us for a moment." Resist the urge to make your anger the consequence. Instead, confidently hold your child accountable for his or her behavior (with a verbal or a determined consequence), if needed.

When you feel insecure and unsure what to do, ask God for help right away. Focus on experiencing security and gaining knowledge in His leadership.

Resist Judgment and Embrace Grace

Because we deal with our children day in and day out, it becomes very easy to see them through a filter of shortcomings. These techniques are

. . . .

helpful for stopping the Perfection Infection from spreading further into your heart.

Resist the urge to label your child ("She's my difficult child," or "This one pushes my buttons nonstop"). One mom replaced negatives labels with this statement: "She's got a lot of great qualities. They are just challenging qualities to parent." That little change in how you think and talk about your child can root out judgment and keep grace in your heart.

The next time your child does something wrong, work to think of this as a "brain growing" opportunity. Remind yourself that this is a normal part of the natural maturing process. Resist the urge to react with anger, and choose to respond with love, leadership, and grace.

Ask God to show you where you judge yourself or your child unconsciously. When you become aware of it, thank God for the awareness, apologize for the judging spirit in your heart, and ask God to help you see yourself or your child through His eyes of love and grace.

EMBRACE YOUR BEAUTIFUL, IMPERFECT CHILD

Have you ever thought about some of the greatest people in history and who they were as children? Ray Kroc—the founder of McDonald's—was a high school dropout. Thomas Edison—the inventor of the lightbulb—was kicked out of school because he was easily distracted. Henry Ford—the inventor of the automobile—disappointed his father because he did not take over the family farm. Ben Cohen—of Ben and Jerry's ice cream—attended and dropped out of several colleges.[3] All these men have changed our world in some way. The mischief, challenges, and difficulties faced in childhood all contributed to the way God chose to use them.

There are no perfect kids—just unique ones who make mistakes along the way and are wonderful just the way God made them.

Notes

1. Jill Savage and Pam Farrel, *Got Teens?* (Eugene, OR: Harvest House, 2005), 15.
2. Kasey Johnson, "Sidewalk Sprinkler," Smarter Moms (blog), October 20, 2011, http://smartermoms.wordpress.com.
3. Brett and Kate McKay, "25 of the Greatest Self-Made Men in American History," Art of Manliness, December 12, 2008, http://artofmanliness.com.

CHAPTER 4

NO MORE *Perfect* BODIES

I walked out on the stage at a Moms Night Out session of a Hearts at Home conference. Our conference theme for that particular year was Real Moms . . . Real Lives . . . Real Stories. I decided to be real when it came to body challenges.

I invited my very pregnant daughter, Anne, on stage with me. I talked about how I love the new style of maternity clothes that "embrace the baby bump." Sixteen years ago when I was last pregnant, pregnant women wore tents. I shared how I loved that these new styles accentuated the beautiful miracle growing inside.

Then I issued the challenge: Our culture has finally embraced the baby bump. Now it's time for us to start a movement called "Embrace the post-baby baby bump." I turned to the side and let my "post-baby

baby bump" proudly show. No slimmer. No sucking in. No Spanx. Three thousand moms went wild.

Oh, the challenges of the female body! If you became a mom via pregnancy, you know that those little ones stretch your body in more ways than you ever thought possible! Even if you arrived at motherhood via adoption, you've still probably discovered that the female body faces its fair share of challenges. Hormones that rage and a metabolism that slows with age cause most of us, in some way, to struggle with our body images. Add in our culture's "worship" of a thin body and Hollywood's obsession with perfect-looking television and movie stars, and you'll find yourself set up for unfair comparisons.

COMPARE APPLES TO APPLES

If you, like most moms, find yourself feeling insecure about your body image, your weight, your stretch marks, or your flabbiness, you are probably comparing apples to oranges: your body up against the Photoshopped, airbrushed photos of famous people or models. When we make that comparison, you and I will always come up short. Real bodies just don't look like that.

Let's compare apples to apples. My belly could honestly double as a tic-tac-toe board. With vertical stripes of stretch marks and horizontal surgical scars, my belly certainly doesn't look like any body I've seen in magazines or on television. Those stretch marks aren't confined to my belly. They're also evident on my upper legs, my sides, and my rear end. Can you relate?

Then, there are the skin issues. Adult acne often takes over my upper back and occasionally creeps onto my chest and face. When I don't wear foundation, my skin is blotchy and uneven. Wrinkles are showing up around my eyes and mouth—and on my hands. Who would have thought! Do you deal with those kinds of skin challenges?

Then there are the varicose veins. Some moms develop these in their twenties, and others start finding them in their thirties and forties. Long and sometimes squiggly blue/green lines run vertically up parts of my leg. I sure haven't seen that on any actress or magazine model! Surely I'm not the only one dealing with this!

Okay, let's go further. Four years of braces straightened my teeth, but some have gone crooked again in adulthood (guess I should have been better about wearing my retainer. Sorry, Mom!). Those teeth are also not nearly as white as they used to be. In fact, remember the magazine cover I told you I was on once? One of the "edits" they made to the photo was whitening my teeth. Yep, if you saw that cover and compared your teeth to mine, it would have been an unfair comparison: My teeth aren't that white.

How about your hair? What challenges do you deal with? Oily? Dry? Too thin? Too thick? Too curly? Too fine? Too frizzy? Too coarse? My hair is thick and coarse. When I get it cut, my beautician has to use the thinning shears until her hand hurts. Then I shed for days after a haircut!

Of course, there are the weight issues. Where do you gain weight? All over? In your rear and thighs? In your belly? That's where I gain weight. It's a constant battle for me and has been for years (thus my promotion about embracing the "post-baby baby bump!")

If that's not enough, I'm blind as a bat without my glasses or contacts. I have something called "geographic tongue," which means I have weird looking spots on my tongue. I also have fibromyalgia, which causes intense physical pain and exhaustion during flare-ups. Then there's the IBS—Irritable Bowel Syndrome—that I've dealt with for years and a bladder issue that makes me pee every time I sneeze or cough!

Your body is really more "normal" than you thought.

Maybe your body issues are more serious or debilitating. My friend Jeralyn deals with rheumatoid arthritis. Another friend, Carla, now walks with a walker and deals with intense pain after her body was mangled in a car accident.

I bet you saw yourself in some of those descriptions. You could add challenges you deal with that I haven't mentioned here. The things you might add would make another mom feel better about her body because she'd know she's not alone in those struggles. You see, when we compare insides to insides, we find out our bodies are really more "normal" than we thought. This discovery is the first step in learning to love the very real bodies God has given us.

WHAT DOES GOD THINK?

When you look at yourself in the mirror, what filter do you see yourself through? Do you compare what you see in the mirror to what you see in magazine and television articles? Or do you see yourself through God's eyes? His eyes care more about the condition of your heart than the condition of your skin. We can make peace with our bodies if we will learn to see it through God's eyes. Let's explore what God says about our bodies and our hearts.

First Corinthians 6:19–20 asks, "Do you not know that your body is a temple of the Holy Spirit within you, whom you have from God? You are not your own, for you were bought with a price. So glorify God in your body" (ESV). A little earlier in 1 Corinthians we read, "Do you not know that you are God's temple and that God's Spirit dwells in you? . . . For God's temple is holy, and you are that temple (1 Corinthians 3:16–17 ESV). From the book of Romans comes this instruction: "I appeal to you . . . present your bodies as a living sacrifice, holy and acceptable to God" (Romans 12:1 ESV). First Corinthians also reminds us, "So, whether you eat or drink, or whatever you do, do all to the glory of God" (1 Corinthians 10:31 ESV). All of these verses tell us that our bodies belong to God. He asks us to take care of our bodies and treat them like the Holy Spirit's precious home. So taking care of our physical bodies is a stewardship issue. We are taking care of something that doesn't actually belong to us, but instead belongs to God.

When you consider these verses, do you get the feeling that your body is actually a gift from God? I do. In fact, it's a gift God made Himself! In Psalm 139 we discover, "For you created my inmost being; you knit me together in my mother's womb. I praise you because I am fearfully and wonderfully made; your works are wonderful, I know that full well (Psalm 139:13–14).

Have you ever toiled and labored intensely to make a gift? I have! What immediately comes to mind are the T-shirt quilts I made for my son and son-in-law one Christmas. My son's quilt was made from fifteen T-shirts and my son-in-law's was a double-sided quilt with forty T-shirts! I cut, ironed, and sewed until I was dreaming about T-shirts. The forty-T-shirt quilt required two people to manage the bulk of material that had to be guided through the sewing machine. Without the help of my mother and my husband, I would never have finished that thing! When

I presented these quilts to the boys on Christmas Day, I announced to them, "If you EVER wonder if I love you, just look at these quilts. They are evidence of much sacrifice and a heart full of love for you."

Now imagine God knitting together your body. When the last stitch is complete, He says, "If you EVER wonder if I love you, just look at this incredible body I've given you. It is evidence of sacrifice and a heart full of love for you." Our bodies are truly miraculous. The body, this incredible gift, contains more than 300 million capillaries in the lungs alone! Not only that, but each kidney in your body contains a million individual filters that filter blood and urine. Did you know the bones in your body are as strong as granite for supporting weight? In fact, a block of bone the size of a matchbox can support nine tons—four times more than concrete can support! And talk about efficiency: A single human blood cell can complete a circuit of the entire body in just about sixty seconds.[1] The human body is an intricate piece of artwork God fashioned and gave to each one of us. Think about that the next time you stand in front of a mirror and want to start critiquing your body!

ENJOY THE GIFT OF YOUR BODY

When I gave my son and son-in-law their quilts, the only thing I hoped they would do was enjoy the gift I'd made and take care of it. God wants the same from us: to enjoy the gift of our bodies and take care of them. You and I can do that by moving, resting, hydrating, and feeding our bodies.

Move It!

Exercise is an essential aspect of taking care of our bodies. There are two kinds of exercise we need to be doing: cardio fitness and strength building. The good news is that you don't need a gym membership to do either one! Aerobic exercise not only burns calories but keeps your heart healthy and strong. Thirty to forty-five minutes of cardiac exercise can happen when you take a walk with a girlfriend or walk alongside your kids as they take a bike ride. In addition to four-to-six days a week of cardio, make sure you get in two or three days a week of strength training. Strength training can happen with muscle building exercises like sit-ups, push-ups, lifting weights, kettlebells, and resistance bands. Strength training burns calories, increases metabolism, increases bone density, strengthens muscles, and improves balance. Got some soup cans in your pantry? Pull some out and start lifting today!

Rest It!

Our bodies are designed to regenerate during sleep. When we sleep, the immune system is strengthened, hormones that regulate the appetite are released, and the brain and body are allowed the rest needed for memory and general fitness. Sleep is for the body like a reboot is for a computer. It clears away the junk so you function better. If you are up at night with a baby, don't hesitate to take a nap during the day if you can. If you're not getting seven to nine hours of sleep each night, it's time to hit the sack earlier (for most moms, getting up later just isn't an option!). Even going to sleep thirty minutes earlier than your usual bedtime can make a difference in taking care of this gift God has given you!

Hydrate It!

Did you know that many headaches are a symptom of dehydration? It's definitely better for our bodies to drink a glass of water rather than run

....

for the medicine cabinet. I don't personally like the taste of plain water, so I've discovered that if I throw in a slice of lemon, lime, orange, or even cucumber, I'm more likely to drink the water I need. I have one friend who drinks her water out of a beautiful stemware glass from her china cabinet. She says that drinking her water out of such a pretty goblet is a simple way to "treat" herself to something special! Remember the "8 x 8" rule: Drink eight ounces of water eight times a day. This keeps your energy up and your body functioning well.

Feed It!

Most of us have no problem feeding our bodies. The challenge is feeding it healthy foods. It's so easy to go through the fast-food drive-thru and consider that a check next to "Feed myself" on the to-do list. At home we might throw hot dogs on the stove and whip up boxed mac and cheese. Those choices are fine on occasion, but they need to be the exception and not the rule. Keep fresh fruit and vegetables on hand to serve with meals and munch on for snacks. Read labels and choose foods that don't have preservatives or large amounts of sodium in them. Opt for lean meats like turkey over ground beef. Limit sweets to special occasions, rather than making them something to eat every day. Select water or tea over soda. Limit the amount of artificial sweeteners you are using. Making these small adjustments can help you feed your body with the healthy food it needs.

WHAT ABOUT THE HEART?

God has given us these incredible physical bodies to live in on this earth, and He wants us to take care of them. However, God is more concerned about the condition of our hearts than anything else. We see evidence of that in the book of Samuel, which describes how God told Samuel this very powerful truth, "For the Lord sees not as man sees: man looks on the outward appearance, but the Lord looks on the heart" (1 Samuel 16:7 ESV).

So what is it that God looks at when He sees our hearts? Does that mean God is concerned about the organ with atria and ventricles that pumps blood through our physical bodies? No, not in this instance. The heart God is talking about is the core of who we are: our thoughts, beliefs, emotions, and desires. Our hearts determine our priorities, obedience, faithfulness, and loyalty. The heart can be hard and un-yielding to God or it can be soft, pliable, and able to be influenced by God. This is what God is looking for when He looks at our hearts. When God whispers to us, do we obey or disobey? When faced with a tough situation, do we choose God's way or insist on our own way? Are we characterized by pride or humility? Anger or forgiveness? Criticism or grace? Fear or courage? All of these are by-products of the condition of our hearts. They are the fruit (good or bad) in our lives.

The Bible talks about the good fruit in the book of Galatians where the term *fruit of the Spirit* is used. First, the book of Galatians describes the battle between "flesh" and "spirit." This isn't referring to the literal flesh on our bodies; it is referring to doing things our way instead of God's way: "So I say, walk by the Spirit, and you will not gratify the desires of the flesh. For the flesh desires what is contrary to the Spirit, and the Spirit what is contrary to the flesh. They are in conflict with each other, so that you are not to do whatever you want" (Galatians 5:16–17).

Then God goes on to outline what "walking in the flesh" looks like:

....

"The acts of the flesh are obvious: sexual immorality, impurity and de-bauchery; idolatry and witchcraft; hatred, discord, jealousy, fits of rage, selfish ambition, dissensions, factions and envy; drunkenness, orgies, and the like" (Galatians 5:19–21). There are a few things on that list I don't have too many problems with, but I admit that I can be prone to "walk in the flesh" when it comes to idolatry (thinking about some-thing more than God), jealousy, fits of rage (like when the Mommy Monster shows up), selfish ambition, dissensions (picking an argument with my husband), and envy. Can you relate to any of those?

The beautiful thing is that God doesn't leave us without a vision of what He longs for us to experience. He casts this vision in verses 22–23 and 26: "But the fruit of the Spirit is love, joy, peace, forbearance [pa-tience], kindness, goodness, faithfulness, gentleness and self-control . . . Since we live by the Spirit, let us keep in step with the Spirit. Let us not become conceited, provoking and envying each other." What He's saying here is that when we live life God's way, we will experience some wonderful results like patience, peace, joy, and self-control. Who among us hasn't prayed for those things?

This is where tending to the inside (heart) fits with tending to the outside (body). Many of us wish for more self-control when it comes to eating or exercising, and we often tackle that with a "change of habit" strategy. Unfortunately, that change of habit is often short-lived. Why? Because we're trying to make an external change without getting to the heart of the issue — literally. In Proverbs 4:23 we read, "Keep your heart with all vigilance, for from it flow the springs of life" (ESV). The fruits of the Spirit all bring life to us in some way. By allowing God to lead, we open up the "springs of life" and find freedom from being controlled

. . . .

by our desires, our idols, our anger, our demands, and our pursuit of the things of this world.

Lysa TerKeurst addresses this in her bestselling book *Made to Crave* when she says, "Getting healthy isn't just about losing weight. It's not limited to adjusting our diet and hoping for good physical results. It's about recalibrating our souls so that we want to change—spiritually, physically, and mentally."[2] I love the phrase *recalibrating our souls*. So often our body issues reflect what is going on inside of us. So we try to change our habits, we promise to exercise, we declare we will eat healthier, we pledge to go to bed earlier, but none of that works in the long run. Maybe our promise to exercise is actually blocked by a fear of failure. Our desire to eat healthier doesn't stick because we use food to comfort us instead of simply providing us nutrition. Our pledge to go to bed earlier is circumvented by our pride that says, "I have so much on my plate because I'm the only one who can really do all of these tasks well."

So we often try to change our outward behavior when we really need to focus on the issues in our hearts that produce these behaviors. That's why God says that while humans look at the outward appearance, He looks at the heart. God knows that the heart is the wellspring of life. It is the core of who we are. Therefore, if we're going to make peace with our imperfect bodies, we have to start with tending to our hearts.

APPLY THE ANTIDOTE

When it comes to loving our bodies, we could apply any or all of the four antidotes we've been talking about depending on what heart issues we're dealing with. However, for more general purposes, let's apply the two antidotes that would apply to most of us: confidence and grace.

....

Move from Insecurity to Confidence

The insecurity most of us feel about our bodies is based on how we view our bodies and who or what we are comparing them to. You and I move from insecurity to confidence when we are able to see our bodies from God's perspective.

If you'd really like to recover from the Perfection Infection as it pertains to your body, you'll need to do some work. Try these two practical strategies to apply the antidotes to your real life:

Write down some of the Bible verses shared earlier in this chapter on index cards. Place those cards in places where you'll be sure to see them, like your bathroom mirror or your refrigerator door. You can even use a dry erase marker and actually write a verse on a mirror. This will grow your God-fidence—confidence found through God's truth.

Thank God for your many parts. One day after your shower, stand in front of a full length mirror completely naked. Starting with your feet, talk to God about each part of your body saying only positive things and nothing negative. You might start with, "God, I thank you for my feet. Some people can't use their feet, but I can. Thank you for the support they provide for my body." Keep doing that until you get to the top of your head, "This is my hair. It's brown and quite thick. I also have a cowlick on the right side of my forehead. This makes me unique." Repeat this exercise as often as you can, verbally accepting and saying something affirming about each part of your body. Cultivating a heart of gratitude will change your perspective and help you move from insecurity to confidence about your body.

. . . .

Shift from Judgment to Grace

The other antidote to apply is grace. We are our own worst critics. We sit in judgment of ourselves, constantly seeing only through our eyes that continually compare. However, God sees us not through eyes of judgment, but of grace. We also need to learn to see ourselves through eyes of grace.

God sees us for who we are, not for who we aren't.

When God sees us through eyes of grace, He sees the possibilities, not the liabilities. He sees our strengths, not our weaknesses. He sees us for who we are, not for who we aren't. You and I can learn to do the same. It's not easy, but it is possible. Making peace with your body will silence the critic in your mind.

There are some practical ways to move from judgment to grace.

Pay attention to the self-talk in your head concerning your body. Are there old tapes from childhood or your teen years that surface? A careless comment from an old boyfriend or a previous relationship that's never left you? Without realizing it, we still use those messages to define ourselves. When you identify one of those messages, call it what it is: a lie. Ask God to replace that lie with His truth. (See appendix A for truth about who you are.) If those messages are deep-seated, don't hesitate to pursue Christian counseling. Remember, caring for yourself emotionally is just as important as caring for your physical body.

When judgment surfaces, attach a reason and a sense of gratefulness to the issue being criticized. For instance, when I see my zebra-striped stomach, I tell myself, "I have stretch marks because I gave birth to four beautiful children. During those pregnancies I gained weight to give life to those children. Thank you, God, for giving me that opportunity." You're not using it as an excuse but simply reminding yourself of the

. . . .

"why" behind the troublesome issue.

Tend to your heart before you tend to your body. If you decide you want to change something about your body, work from the inside out. Anything done without God is done in vain. Tell God your desires. Ask Him to search your heart and call to your attention anything that gets in the way of you caring for your body. You might pray something like, "God, I want to take care of this body You've given me. I'd like to get closer to a healthy weight for my height. Can You help me see what I need to tend to in my heart so that I can be successful in taking care of my body?"

EMBRACE YOUR BEAUTIFUL, IMPERFECT BODY

Have you ever considered all that we put our bodies through? Think about the added weight of pregnancy or just the added weight of aging. What about carrying around a baby on your hip? Making your breasts the primary food source for a baby? Crawling with your little one on the floor? We lift, bend, stretch, and hold positions until our backs hurt terribly. We lose sleep and carry stress. We put dozens of miles on our feet. We give thousands of baths with our hands. Our bodies allow us to hug, smile, and wipe away the tears of those we love.

There are no perfect bodies—but we each have one that serves us better than we often realize.

Notes

1. "Top 15 Amazing Facts About the Human Body," adapted from *The Reader's Digest Book of Facts*, posted on Listverse, June 10, 2008, http://listverse.com.
2. Lysa TerKeurst, *Made to Crave* (Grand Rapids: Zondervan, 2012), 16.

CHAPTER 5

NO MORE *Perfect* MARRIAGES

Dear Jill,

I'm weary. I'm frustrated. It feels that my husband and I disagree more often than we agree, especially now that we have kids. Everybody else seems madly in love. I see pictures of couples and families on Facebook and on people's blogs. I guess there are pictures on my blog that look good, too. But the truth is they don't communicate the reality that marriage is hard work, and sometimes I'm not feeling like "happily ever after" is real. Am I the only one who feels this way?

Amanda

. . . .

Dear Amanda,

No, you are not the only one who feels that way. Marriage
is hard at times and it is definitely hard work. Welcome
to the real world: There are no perfect marriages.

Jill

Thus began a Facebook conversation I had with a mom one summer evening. Our expectations of the perfect love story set us up for failure when the real challenges of marriage surface. After all, most of us were brought up on Disney movies. We dreamed of a handsome prince finding us, sweeping us off our feet, and riding off with him into the sunset.

Even the best of marriages face challenges when children enter the scene. Values are challenged, differences become evident, sleep is deprived, tempers run short, upbringings clash, and life is just plain old chaotic. Real marriages face real challenges. If you've been like Amanda—comparing the insides of your marriage to the outsides of other marriages—an honest discussion is needed so you can better understand real married life and the real challenges we all face.

1 + 1 = 14

The first challenge every marriage faces is the merging of two families of origin. From the start, a new couple is blending the deeply embedded family patterns and traditions from two separate families. Maybe one family handled conflict by pretending it didn't exist. Conversely, the spouse's family handled conflict by yelling and screaming. One family handled parenting by giving lots of freedom to the children. The spouse's family ran a tight ship with lots of rules and boundaries in place. One family made a big deal of birthdays with lots of gifts and celebrations, while the other family just honored the birthday person with words of encouragement but little festivity. One family went to church every Sunday, while the other family attended only on Easter and Christmas.

Mark and I ran into this within one month of saying, "I do." It was Mark's twenty-third birthday, and I planned a celebration the way my family celebrated birthdays: a homemade cake, a homemade meal, and a house full of relatives. I found out very quickly that wasn't how birthdays were celebrated in Mark's family. According to Mark, we were supposed to go out to eat, have a store-bought cake with little candy letters on it that spelled out HAPPY BIRTHDAY, and friends and family were supposed to be invited. How was I supposed to know that all these years my family had been wrong?

Birthdays were just the beginning. There were differences in summer vacations, Christmas, and Easter. According to each of us, there was a "right" way to grill, to make chili, to manage money, and to clean a bathroom. There was even a "right" way to put the toilet paper roll on the toilet roll dispenser. Of course, we rarely agreed on what the right way was because our "rights" were completely different from each other's!

Not only did habits and traditions collide, but suddenly there were more than two people in this new relationship. He brought his family into our new union and I brought my family into this relationship, too. 1 + 1 did not equal 2. It appeared to equal more than a dozen people! Is this what is meant by for better or for worse?

. . . .

Every marriage faces the challenge of blending two families. Without realizing it, we both come into marriage with expectations that this new family we will be forming will do things the same way the family we came from did things. Ah! There's that *expectation* word again. It gets us in trouble every time, doesn't it?

If you've found yourself disagreeing with your spouse about communication, parenting, sex, money, or which way the toilet paper roll goes on the toilet paper dispenser, you are not alone. Those are common challenges in marriage. It's hard work to blend two lives, two perspectives, two sets of experiences, and, of course, two sets of expectations!

If you've ever found yourself disillusioned with the real stuff of marriage, dealing with baggage from the seemingly incompatible families you came from, you are among friends. Most of us have experienced that feeling. It doesn't mean it's time to throw in the towel. It doesn't mean you aren't compatible. It doesn't mean you haven't found your soul mate. It simply means you're normal—absolutely normal.

Real marriage isn't what you see in the sitcoms.

THE HARD WORK OF MARRIAGE

Marriage is hard work. There's no getting around it. At first, most of us found the statement "Love is blind" to be true. Those differences were fascinating—at least in the beginning. Our horizons were expanded by this new family connection, and we found the new experiences to be charming. In time, however, the challenges were, well . . . challenging!

Real marriage isn't what you see in the sitcoms, it's not what you watch at the movies, and it's definitely not the stuff romance novels are made of. Certainly, there are elements in those that we can relate to.

. . . .

Unfortunately, however, the media more often establishes unrealistic expectations—even fantasies—of what a loving, married relationship should look like.

If we're honest, real marriage brings our "yuck" to the surface. Selfishness and pride raise their ugly heads in the everyday life of a normal marriage. After all, we like things the way we like them. Our way *is* the right way. Our rationale is always more logical than our spouse's rationale. Right?

In his book *Sacred Marriage,* author Gary Thomas poses this question: What if God designed marriage to make us holy more than to make us happy?[1] Now that is a question that will mess with your mind. Think about it a bit, though. You put two very different people in the same family, same house, and even the same bed, and then you ask them suddenly to begin to sleep together, make decisions together, raise children together, and navigate the twists and turns of life together. That's a recipe for conflict right there.

It's in the living together of everyday life that our ugly stuff comes out. If we're willing to look, we are suddenly able to see how selfish we really are. Our human nature wants always to have things our way. That's the core of selfishness. When we care only about ourselves or our own needs, we shut our spouse's needs out. How does this selfishness play out in everyday life? It may be in ways you've never even considered. For instance, if you are sitting at the computer typing an email when your husband walks in the door from being gone all day, do you stop what you are doing, leave your chair, and greet him with a kiss? If not, then selfishness just reigned. You cared more about the task you were trying to accomplish than the person walking in the door. Ouch, that hurts, doesn't it?

We are by nature selfish people. However, God showed us another way. He modeled for us the servant life when He sent His Son, Jesus, to earth. Jesus served. He washed feet. He spent time with people when there was something else on His "to do" list. He ultimately gave His life for ours. That is the most unselfish act someone can do. God gives us direction for living sacrificially in Philippians 2:3–5: "Do nothing out of selfish ambition or vain conceit. Rather, in humility value others above yourselves, not looking to your own interests but each of you to the interests of the others."

I would venture to say that most moms have less of a problem living this out with their children than they do with their husbands. We expect something different from him than we do from our children. After all our children are, well, *children*. But a husband, well, he's an adult. He is responsible for more. More is expected from him. Could it be that this is the message we're harboring deep inside our hearts at times: "My husband is an adult. He's supposed to be serving me just like I'm supposed to be serving him. If he isn't holding up his end of the bargain, why should I uphold my end of the bargain?" Ahh—selfishness rises up again. We all struggle with it in some form or another. But there's something else that makes marriage hard work. It's the "yuck" of pride.

Pride is at the core of so much marital strife. Pride believes our way is the right way—the only way. Pride says that *you* are more wrong than I am. Pride says I'm not wrong at all. Pride says that an apology would be a sign of weakness. Pride keeps conflict from being resolved and love from being shown.

Perfect marriages don't exist because they are made up of two imperfect people. Unfortunately, pride keeps us from admitting just how imperfect we are. God tells us, "Pride goes before destruction, a haughty spirit before a fall" (Proverbs 16:18). Apply that to marriage, and we're reminded that pride will destroy a marriage. That's some powerful truth. Why then do we struggle with pride? Control. We falsely believe we are protecting ourselves by keeping "control" of a situation rather than serving or submitting to our spouse. We falsely believe we need to keep the upper hand in our relationship so no one—not even our spouse—can take advantage of us. We falsely believe that our ways are the only right ways and we have to stay in control of things so they are done correctly.

Do you have trouble admitting any of those things? It's probably pride getting in the way once again. We don't want to admit we're wrong, sinful, or have impure motives in any way. Let's be honest: If you're human, you struggle with pride. There are no perfect marriages, because there are no perfect people making up the union of two lives.

IT'S UNHUMANABLE!

What do we do with the selfishness and pride stuff that clutters up our hearts? To begin with we go back to the heart of Gary Thomas's question. We allow marriage to prompt us to pursue holiness, to deepen our spiritual walk, to make us more like Christ.

Do you want to be happy? The way to "happy" is holiness. Pursue holiness—seriously. Let me share with you how I have experienced, this past year, the truth of how happiness is a by-product of seeking after holiness.

In July 2011, my husband began to enter a deep pit of depression and disillusionment. He was not attentive to my needs or the needs of the family. He was wrapped up in his own world of lies the enemy was feeding him. I kept asking God what to do, and I knew God's answer was, "I want you to love him." I would say to God, "I don't know if you've noticed, but he's a bit unlovable right now." And God would respond in the depth of my soul, "Well, I don't know if you've noticed, but you've been a bit unlovable yourself at times." So I asked God to show me how to love my husband in his depression. During this season I drew so close to God that it felt as if I was asking Him what to do every step of the day. I just didn't have the energy or the knowledge to know how to love someone who was being so unloving to me. However, God showed me each and every step. When Mark communicated sharply, I would respond with a soft answer. When Mark put distance between us, I would draw closer to him by praying for him. When he rejected me and walked out the door, I asked God to show me how to stand my ground with necessary boundaries but still show him the love God was asking me to show him. Sure, there were times I blew it. My flesh fought with God's Spirit. But I'd ask for forgiveness and move forward in His grace.

During the time when Mark was living elsewhere, he would ask me out to dinner once a week. He said it was for the purpose of communication, not restoration. Each time I'd go into the dinner in an attitude of prayer, "God, this is too big for me. You have to do the loving. Just let me be the vessel." One evening Mark broke and said, "How can you treat me so kindly when I have treated you so badly?" Without thinking I said, "It's only because of God, Mark. It's unhumanable." He laughed at my made-up word. I laughed at it, too. I don't actually know where that word came from. It exited my mouth without me even thinking about it. However, it was a perfect description of what was happening in me.

I was pursuing holiness, and God was giving me what I needed when I needed it. It was absolutely an un-human experience. My flesh wanted to lash out at my husband, but my heart was being controlled by my God, who is more powerful. I just had to be willing.

But that's not all. I was still able to find peace and joy in the midst of such a horrible time. Don't get me wrong. I cried my heart out. There were days I was not functional enough to make a meal for my boys. I was brokenhearted and deeply wounded by the actions of my husband. However, because I was drawing close to God in the midst of it, I found truth in the words that Jennifer Rothschild had shared at our 2010 Hearts at Home conferences: "It may not be well with my circumstances, but it is well with my soul." I knew, without a doubt, that in the midst of my

God is still God even when we are ungodly.

changing circumstances, my God did not change. There is peace and joy in that truth. It provided a sense of calm in the midst of my horrible circumstances. I knew I would be okay even if my husband didn't return to our home and family. I didn't want that to happen. In fact, I never stopped believing in my marriage. However, I knew that God was still God even when we are ungodly in our actions. Knowing that God's love, provision, and protection would not change even if my husband's love, provision, and protection did change, gave me a sense of contentment that was quite unhumanable, as well.

There is a happy ending to this story. My husband did return home repentant and remorseful for the pain he had caused. He set up accountability measures with some friends, who began to meet weekly and read the Bible with him. He asked for God's forgiveness and walked in His grace. He asked for my forgiveness and for the forgiveness of our children, our two sons-in-law and our daughter-in-law. He pursued holiness himself, immersing himself in God's truth, setting up boundaries to keep temptation at bay, and sorting through things with a Christian counselor. One day about six weeks into his recommitment to God and family, he texted me, "I just realized something: I'm happy. I'm really, really happy." He, too, was pursuing holiness—and found happiness was a by-product!

What imperfections are you dealing with in your life? Where have selfishness, pride, and other junk in your heart kept you from both holiness and happiness? The unhumanable efforts to live life God's way are where we draw closer to Him than ever before.

HE'S YOUR HUSBAND, NOT YOUR CHILD

The email I received started like so many other emails, conversations, and Facebook messages I've had exchanged with moms over the years. "Dear Jill, I'm a mom of four . . . well, five, if you count my husband . . . " I know I've said it before myself. Most of us have. We say it to interject some humor and maybe even some camaraderie into our conversation with another mom. But have you ever considered how disrespectful and demeaning it is to your husband to categorize him with your children?

If we look at the concept of "expectations" from a different angle, we might see that some of us "expect" our husbands to be irresponsible. Oh, I know, you usually make the flippant comment about your husband being like one of the kids over something trivial: He can't find the ketchup bottle sitting right in the front of the second shelf on the refrigerator—just like the kids. Or you say it because it feels like he forgets to do something he said he would do so you have to do it for him just like you do things for everyone else in the family.

And you don't ever overlook the ketchup or forget details or chores, right?

If I "expect" my husband to act like a child and I "mother" him like a child, I will lose respect for him as my husband. There's a problem with that because God gives us one very big "to do" in our marriage: Respect our husbands (Ephesians 5:33).

The more I get serious about obeying God by respecting my husband, the more I see positive change happening in my marriage. My friend Karen has been challenging me on this issue in her book *The God-Empowered Wife*. When I read these words, they were quite convicting for me:

> We emasculate our husbands by mothering them and then complain they aren't stepping up to the plate. When that doesn't work, we use thinly disguised attempts to control and change them—pushing and prodding them to do what we think they should, or setting a "good example" and hoping they get the hint. Eventually, we end up way out in front, stretched thin trying to pull our husbands forward and wondering why they aren't cooperating... We become the dominant spouse, even if that wasn't our original intent.[2]

Ooooh—that hits a little too close to home for me. Does it for you?

This is the place God has been challenging me lately. I'm realizing that my expectations are once again damaging my relationships, but not because my expectations are too high, rather because they are too low. Those low expectations keep me from giving my husband the respect he deserves.

Sue Bohlin addresses this issue in her tongue-in-cheek article titled "Trash Your Marriage in 8 Easy Steps." Step number 7 is this:

> Wives, *be a mother* to your husband. When people ask how many children you have, say things like, "Two—three, if you count my husband." Tell him to wear a coat when it's cold and take an umbrella when it's raining, because he can't figure it out on his own. Be sure to say, "I told you so" as often as possible. If he is passive or irresponsible, jump in and rescue him so he won't have to deal with the consequences of his own choices. Make sure he feels three years old. Tell him how to live his life, down to the smallest detail.

Bohlin then goes on to say, "What we really mean to say: Please, if you find yourself doing these things, ask for God's help in being *constructive* instead of *destructive*. We want to help you *build* your marriage, not *trash* it."[3]

I'm not alone in this, am I? I think many of us struggle with this line of thinking in our own marriage. You know what I'm learning to do as I work on this imperfection in my marriage? Keep my mouth shut. That's been one of the most important lessons.

THE STUFF NO ONE TALKS ABOUT

Most of us struggle with selfishness and pride in marriage. Most of us find the everyday realities of "respecting" our husbands a difficult challenge. But sometimes the issues go way beyond this fundamental aspect of your relationship. What if you're dealing with bigger stuff than that? What if your marriage has been hurt by pornography, infidelity, or abuse? What if divorce is a part of your story, and *blended family* best describes your family unit? What if you wish marriage were a part of your life but you are instead parenting on your own? What if you and your husband are separated, and the whole topic of marriage is quite painful? What if your husband has lost his job and the bank is threatening to foreclose on your mortgage? What if you live with a man who is highly critical of you or struggles with depression?

When such desperate and difficult issues face you, it's easy to feel completely isolated with that world of trouble. But *you are not alone*. Don't compare the insides of your marriage to the outsides of other people's marriages. Pictures don't tell the truth. Smiling faces on Christmas cards don't reveal the pain behind the scenes. While your struggles are very personal and often very painful, but they are not unique. Many other moms face the difficulties you have had or are facing. The challenge is finding someone who understands. Honestly, today that is easier than ever before. You may not find a mom in your neighborhood or community, but a simple Google search will connect you with websites and blogs hosted by moms dealing with just about any issue out there.

Take Trisha Davis, for instance. She blogs at www.refineus.org with her husband, Justin. After successfully planting their first church, Justin had an affair with a staff member, who was also Trisha's best friend. This couple is now several years down the road from their four-year journey of pain, grief, and ultimately, the restoration of their relationship. They share openly on their blog about restoring a marriage scarred by infidelity.

· · · · · · · ·

At www.laurabwilliams.com, you'll find Laura's somewhat similar story, which gives hope to those who are healing after an affair.

There's www.brokenheartonhold.com, where you'll meet Linda. She and her husband were separated for three years before their marriage was restored. At www.todayschristianwoman.com, look for an excellent article by Cheri Fuller, based upon firsthand experience, about how to handle life when your husband is depressed. If you're a single mom, you might check out www.thelifeofasinglemom.com, where you'll find women who understand. If you're divorced, or "stepmom" is one of your titles, you can find a friend in Laura Petherbridge at www.laurapetherbridge.com.

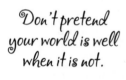

Don't pretend your world is well when it is not.

With so many diverse marriage issues that moms are dealing with, we can't possibly address them all here, but the point is there is help. There are other women who have walked the road you're walking. There are women willing to be honest about the issues it feels like no one is willing to talk about. A comprehensive ministry that can point you in the right direction is Focus on the Family. Dial up 1-800-A-FAMILY and start the conversation with "I'm looking for resources on [insert issue]," and someone will point you to some of the best resources on that topic.

Don't suffer in silence. Don't listen to the enemy's lie that you are the only one dealing with whatever you're dealing with. Don't isolate yourself, put on a mask, and pretend the world is well when it is not. Be honest. Ask for help. Look for resources that will keep you focused on God, grounded in truth, and connected to someone who understands.

There are no perfect wives. There are no perfect husbands. There are no perfect marriages.

········

CHANGE EXPECTATIONS

The statement, "My husband and I are so incompatible!" is an indication of unrealistic expectations. Every married couple is wonderfully incompatible! Sure, some of us share more hobbies, interests, beliefs, and perspectives about life with our spouses than other couples do. However, every couple deals with differences in one way or another. To expect differences not to exist is unrealistic. Change your expectations of what you will need to navigate when it comes to pursuing oneness in your marriage. Expect differences: They will exist, and sometimes they will cause conflict.

That leads us to the next expectation that needs to be adjusted. Conflict is normal. It does happen. It's a natural part of blending two lives. The important thing to do is learn to handle conflict in a godly way. We can't expect our marriages to be conflict-free. That's not realistic. Expect conflict. It will exist and, if you handle it well, it can actually deepen your intimacy.

Expect an ebb and flow of feelings in your marriage. No couple feels "in love" all the time. Feelings breathe, they are fluid, and they don't always tell us the truth. If you feel that you don't love your spouse anymore, recognize that true love is a choice, not a feeling. Increase your loving actions, and your feelings will reignite in time.

Expect to ask for help when your relationship is headed in the wrong direction. When our bodies are sick, we go to a doctor. When our marriages are sick, a Christian counselor can be a huge help in communication and digging down to issues at the core of our challenges. If you don't know where to start, ask for recommendations from your pastor or friends who have found relationship counseling helpful.

· · · · · · · ·

Don't hesitate to change counselors if you feel that one or both of you are not connecting with the counselor you're seeing.

Expect to share your expectations. Your spouse is not a mind reader. He doesn't feel the same way you do. He doesn't think the same way you do. He doesn't make decisions or process hardship the same way you do. If you desire something from him, ask him. *With words.* That conversation will either help you get your needs met or help you see that your expectations are out of line.

I once heard someone say, "Expectations are preconceived resentments." Now that statement stopped me in my tracks. It especially applies to the marriage relationship, where our unmet expectations turn into resentments, which turn into bitterness that turns into anger, and ultimately becomes conflict that could have actually been avoided.

It's okay to expect some realistic things like differences, conflict, and an ebb and flow of feelings. Just be careful not to put your hope in another person by weighing him down with your expectations that he'll act and respond in a certain way. Don't make him responsible for your happiness. Those are the kinds of expectations that lead to resentments that clutter your heart in an unhealthy way.

APPLY THE ANTIDOTE

The Perfection Infection has contaminated marriages just as it's contaminated all the other parts of our lives. The first step in building up a resistance to this damaging ailment is to recognize its existence and its effect on our marriage. Once we can see the reality of marriage, we can begin to apply the antidotes needed.

....

Replace Pride with Humility

There's no other relationship where replacing pride with humility is more important than in marriage. Pride keeps conflict unresolved. It keeps us from owning our own stuff. It keeps us from being willing to see there are other good ways to do things than the way we think is the only right way. Pride separates, hurts, and even destroys.

Humility forms the core of a healthy marriage. Humility helps bring resolve to conflict. It allows us to own our own stuff, no matter how big or small our contributions are to the problem. Humility allows us to see that other people have good ideas. Humility unites, heals, and builds up. If you need to replace pride with humility in your heart, you'll find one or more of these strategies helpful:

Own your own stuff. Even if your spouse is 90 percent wrong and you are only 10 percent wrong, apologize for your 10 percent and ask for forgiveness—regardless of whether your spouse owns his part or not. You and I are only responsible for the condition of our hearts and our obedience to God.

Look at what God says about pride. If you go to www.biblegateway. com and search the word *pride*, you'll find that more than sixty verses deal with pride. I would say that makes it a big deal. These verses from the book of Proverbs help us understand why we need to deal with pride: "I hate pride and arrogance, evil behavior and perverse speech" (8:13), "When pride comes, then comes disgrace, but with humility comes wisdom" (11:2), "Where there is strife, there is pride, but wisdom is found in those who take advice" (13:10), "A fool's mouth lashes out with pride, but the lips of the wise protect them" (14:3), and "Pride goes before destruction, a haughty spirit before a fall" (16:18).

Practice humility. *Humility* comes naturally to some people, but usually it needs to be learned. Start by deferring to your husband when something really doesn't matter. For instance, if he suggests you go to a Mexican restaurant for dinner when you were thinking Italian, just agree to Mexican with a joyful heart. With humility, we accept our place as one person in a marriage of two or one person in a family of five. When we recognize that we are no more important than anyone else, it allows us to replace pride with humility.

Replace Fear with Courage

Fear keeps us from being honest, which keeps emotional intimacy at bay. Courage keeps us honest and deepens the intimacy in marriage. Fear breeds insecurity. Courage brings out confidence. Here are some practical ways to replace fear with courage:

Identify the root of your fears. Are you afraid of rejection? Were you conditioned to be dishonest about your feelings in your home of origin? Do you want to please people so much that you are unable to be honest? Are you afraid of being criticized? Once you are able to identify what is at the core of your fear, you'll better understand the motivation behind your actions. Share your discovery with your spouse and ask him to help you replace fear with courage in your interactions with him.

Take a risk. Are you afraid to tell your husband how you really feel about something? Take a risk and honestly answer a question your husband asks or share with him something you're thinking. Focus on the courage God gives you, not the fear you are feeling. The more risks you take, you'll begin to discover how much you mentally "awfulize" things that never come to fruition. Your fear will decrease and your courage will increase.

Evaluate your fears. On a piece of paper, make five columns. In the first column, list the things that scare you the most. In the second column, for each of those fears, write down what is the absolute worst thing that could happen if your fears came true. Then in the third column, write down how likely the worst thing is to happen. In the next column, write down how that fear is holding you back. Finally, in the last column, *for one or two of the fears you've listed,* write down how you are going to face that fear. Give yourself a practical action to take and a specific date by which you will take that action. Now follow through and watch your courage grow.

Replace Insecurity with Confidence

Insecurity in a marriage causes us to expect our spouse to meet needs that only God can meet. It's important to need our spouse, but equally important to need him in a healthy, balanced way.

Insecurity can also cause us to impose our fears on our spouse. We can ruminate and worry over something so hard and so long that we actually begin to believe it has actually happened—when in reality it hasn't. Consider these if you need to move from insecurity to confidence in your marriage:

Evaluate emotional baggage you might have carried into your marriage. For instance, did your dad desert your family when you were a child? Are you subconsciously waiting for your husband to do the same thing? If you can understand where your insecurity comes from, you're more likely to be able to address it successfully.

Seek counseling. Sometimes our insecurities are deep enough that we need help to understand them. A few sessions with a licensed Christian counselor can help you move insecurity out of your heart.

Read the book How We Love *by Milan and Kay Yerkovich* (Waterbrook). This book helps you understand what a "secure" relationship connection looks like. It also helps us understand how family of origin affects our love relationships.

Replace Judgment with Grace

This is one of the most important antidotes to apply in marriage. Every one of us harbors judgment in our hearts at one time or another. Judging especially raises its ugly head in our marriages when we think thoughts like, *He's so stupid. Can't he get it right?* or *I swear he's just like one of the kids.* Or *He's so irresponsible.* Try these strategies to replace judgment with grace:

Pay attention to your thought life. The Bible says, "Above all else, guard your heart, for everything you do flows from it" (Proverbs 4:23). Your head and your heart work together to determine attitude and behavior. The minute you think something judgmental about your husband, tell God you're sorry and replace the thought with something honoring to your husband.

. . . .

Give grace space. When you give grace to your husband, you allow him to be human, to make mistakes without being criticized all the time. Grace recognizes that we all make mistakes. God gives us grace when we don't deserve it. Give your husband grace when he doesn't deserve it.

EMBRACE YOUR BEAUTIFUL, IMPERFECT HUSBAND

If you are married, thank God right now. There are millions of moms doing this motherhood thing alone. Thank God for your husband's strengths, and work to affirm him for something each and every day. Don't let the Perfection Infection and unrealistic expectations rob you of what you do have.

There are no perfect husbands—just imperfect men who make mistakes along the way and give you the opportunity to learn to love in ways you never knew you could.

Notes

1. Gary Thomas, *Sacred Marriage* (Grand Rapids: Zondervan, 2002).
2. Karen Haught, *The God-Empowered Wife* (Booksurge, 2007), 66.
3. Sue Bohlin, "Trash Your Marriage in 8 Easy Steps," Probe Ministries, 2003, www.probe.org.

CHAPTER 6

NO MORE *Perfect* FRIENDS

It was the day before Anne's sixth birthday. I had promised her a Barbie Doll cake—the kind where the dress of the Barbie is the cake—for her birthday party. Seven-week-old Erica had been sick for a few days, and I decided it was time to take her to the doctor. Upon examination, our pediatrician determined that Erica not only had pneumonia but was also in respiratory distress. This was *not* good for a seven-week-old infant. In the blink of an eye, we were across the street getting checked in to the hospital for what would turn out to be a four-day stay. Because I was nursing Erica, I, too, stayed at the hospital 24/7. Suddenly Anne's need for a Barbie cake took a backseat to a very ill sibling.

One call to my friend Bonnie arranged for Anne's and Evan's pickup from school that day. In order for Mark to be able to be at the hospital

Every mom needs a community of mothers around her.

as much as possible, we decided that the kids would just stay at Bonnie's that first night. In our absence, the next day Anne had the most spontaneous birthday party she'd ever had. Bonnie made her a cake, served it with ice cream, and even presented her with some presents.

Now that's what friends are for!

Every mom needs a community of mothers around her. Those kinds of relationships can be found and fostered in moms groups, churches, neighborhoods, and community groups like the library reading program. My friend Julie and I met that way. We both took our kids to the same reading program at the library. Each week we would enjoy each other's company, and a friendship developed that has lasted over twenty years. Julie has since moved away, but we stay connected on Facebook and get to see each other at the annual Hearts at Home conference in Normal, Illinois, every March. While we weren't the kind of friends who did everything together, our hearts were knit together with similar values and priorities. Now twenty years later, we get to enjoy the grandma season of life together!

Friendships are an important part of mothering. We desperately need each other. However, friendships are not always perfect. If the stories about Bonnie and Julie were all I shared with you, you might assume that everything's always been good in the friendship realm for me. Not true! I've had some great friendships and some not so wonderful friendship experiences. There are no perfect friends, but there are ways we can practice the art of making and being a friend.

THERE YOU ARE!

I once read in a Dear Abby newspaper column that there are two kinds of people in this world: those who walk into a room and say, "Here I am. Come talk to me. Come ask me about me. Come make me feel comfortable," and those who walk into a room and say, "There you are! You look interesting to get to know. Tell me about yourself." It's a subtle but essential distinction.

Friendship has to begin somewhere. If you're friends with someone from childhood, you may not remember how that friendship began. As adults, however, we need to know how to meet someone new, get to know them a bit, and determine if pursuing a friendship would be valuable. The quicker we can learn to be a "There you are!" person, the easier it is to meet new people. When we stay in our "Here I am" corners, we are more concerned about our own comfort level than we are about the comfort of those around us—and we are slow to make friends.

Let's apply this to a real-life situation. Let's say you regularly attend a moms group. You love going each week to see friends, learn something from the guest speaker, and let someone else love on your kids for a couple of hours. One week you see a new face. She's briefly chatted with a few people, but it's obvious she's uncomfortable and doesn't know anyone in the group. You want to approach her but don't really know how best to do that so you don't say anything, talking only to women you know that day. If she says something to you, you'll be happy to chat, but if not . . . oh well.

In that situation, you've completely been a "Here I am" person. You played it safe, but missed out on being Jesus to a person who desperately needed to be seen and valued. You also missed out on meeting someone who may (or may not) become a friend someday.

If she returns to the group the next week, you have another opportunity. This time you decide to put on your courage and be a "There you are!" person. You walk right up to her, offer a firm handshake, and say, "Hi I'm _____, and I don't believe I've had the opportunity to meet you!" She will respond with a handshake and her name. Then you start the "get to know you" discussion: *Tell me about your family. Are you originally from this area? What are the ages of your kids? Do you have a church home? How did you learn about this moms group?* It's not Twenty Questions, but your goal is to learn more about her and, in the process, make her feel welcomed and cared for.

This is how I met my friend Marianne. Her husband was interviewing for a job in our community. Marianne and her two kids came along for the ride to the city. They found a park to play at while Dad went to his interview. It just so happened that our townhouse was right next door to the park. Because my kids were outside playing at the park and I was keeping an eye on them, I had seen her husband drop her and the kids at the park and drive away After a bit of time, one of Marianne's kids announced a need for a bathroom. Knowing there were no public restrooms at the park, I introduced myself to her and told her she was welcome to use our bathroom. During the next hour Marianne and I got to know each other, and a friendship was born. Her husband got the job, and when their family moved to town, she already had a friend. Because our kids were close in age, we eventually traded date nights every week. Marianne and I often got together to let the kids play and enjoy some stimulating conversations ourselves. While we're no longer close friends, we love to reconnect when we run into each other at a store or restaurant, and my life is definitely richer because of the time I spent with Marianne.

So are you a "Here I am" person, or are you a "There you are!" person? Figuring that out will help you know where to start when it comes to meeting new people and launching friendships. For most of us, however, launching friendships isn't where we experience disappointments and frustrations of female relationships. Women's relationships can be an incredible blessing to our lives but, if we're honest, they can also be a source of pain. Since there are no perfect friends, let's explore the realities of friendship challenges.

MEAN GIRLS

I, like you, have my share of "mean girl" stories I can tell. There's the lady who walked up to me at church and announced that my short and spiky hair intimidated her. Then there's the woman who just *had* to be my friend. She emailed and called quite often, and I was really starting to enjoy getting to know her. I thought we were forging a friendship. Then she and her husband decided to change churches, and I suddenly didn't exist anymore. I guess she just wanted to be friends with "the pastor's wife," and not with "Jill."

Then there's the "convenient friend" story. I enjoyed the company of this friend I met through our moms group. We were both stay-at-home moms and lived just a couple of miles apart, which allowed us to get together often to let the kids play. We also traded babysitting quite a bit, which allowed us to go to the store alone or take one child to the doctor without taking all the siblings along. When our family moved to a new home about ten miles across town, suddenly the friendship changed. The requests for trading stopped on her end, and my requests were met with resistance. It seemed the distance was too far to make the friendship realistic. I thought we were real friends, but I guess we were just "convenient friends." Once things weren't convenient, we weren't friends anymore. Then there's the "friend" I had for eight years in my early mothering years. We did everything together, living life to the fullest: laughing together, praying with and for each other, encouraging each other in marriage, parenting, and ministry. Toward the end of our friendship I could tell she was starting to put distance in our relationship, so I asked if I had done something to hurt her. She said no, but the distance continued. I asked again and received the same answer. Finally, one day she asked to meet for coffee, and she told me we couldn't be friends anymore. When I asked why and what had happened, she said "We just can't be friends." To this day, I have no idea what happened in that relationship. What I can tell you, however, is that even now, nearly fifteen years later, I experience deep emotional pain just recounting that story. Although I have forgiven her for the pain she brought to my heart, the truth remains: Imperfect people can hurt us deeply.

You probably have some stories like that. Women's relationships can be a bit complicated. In fact, I didn't really venture into deep female friendships until I became an adult. I didn't have many girlfriends while growing up; I had guy friends. These weren't boyfriends, they were just the guys I played baseball with in the empty lot next to our house or the guys I hung out with in marching band and at school. Guys were safe friends—no backstabbing, no gossip. Of course, the friendships weren't terribly deep—they were just safe. I kind of liked that.

When I became a mom, I realized my need for female relationships.

········

For the first time in my life, I needed other women who understood what my life is like. I was overwhelmed with this new role, and I wanted to know how other moms did it. While I do have a few friends from high school who I stay in touch with, most of the friendships I have today have been forged in adulthood.

So how do we nurture our adult relationships? If we find friends by being a "There you are!" person, how do we move from acquaintance to friend? Let's look at the how-to's of forging friendship and what to do with the frustrations we'll experience at some point with our imperfect friends.

FORGING FRIENDSHIP

I used to tell the women in the moms group I led, "Mom2Mom is where you will meet other moms. Your living room is where you will make friends." I knew these women would never build friendships by simply sitting in the same room with a hundred other women for two hours every Wednesday. Friendship is explored when you invite one of those moms over for peanut butter and jelly sandwiches after the group meeting each week.

Not every mom you invite over will become a close friend, but she will definitely become part of your mothering community. A mothering community comprises women in the same stage of mothering you are. You would stop and chat with them at the grocery store. You might message them on Facebook with a question about potty training or dealing with a rebellious teenager. Your close friends are a part of your mothering community, but so are your acquaintances and other mom friends.

Every once in a while, you'll have a mom over for peanut butter and jelly sandwiches and you'll really click. She'll leave your house, and you'll think, "Wow! That was a lot of fun. I enjoyed her and her kids. I'd like to do that again." If the feeling is mutual, you'll spend time together again—and again and again. A friendship will be born.

A good friend is one you can call at the last minute and say, "Help! I really need some time with my hubby tonight, could my kids come your way for an hour?" Or, "Hey, I've got a sick one I need to take to the doctor. Could you keep my other two?" Of course, friendship is a

Having good friends is like having money in the bank.

two-way street. She has to be able to call you and ask you the same questions, and you need to be willing to reciprocate as needed. A good friend is also one you enjoy meeting for coffee only to find that hours have passed when it felt like minutes.

However, friendships need to be nurtured to be sustainable. In order to keep a friendship healthy, there are some mommy manners we need to know and put into practice. (See *Mommy Manners* on pages 118–19)

FRIENDSHIP FAVORS

Having good friends is like having money in the bank. When life gets rough, they are there when you need to make a withdrawal. When my husband experienced a midlife crisis and walked out the door, three of my closest friends were at my house within the hour. One didn't leave for two days. If she hadn't put food and water in front of me and said, "Eat" and "Drink," I wouldn't have eaten or drunk anything. She accompanied me to a counseling appointment the day after he left, taking notes about things the counselor said, because I couldn't stop crying.

I walked around in a daze for weeks after he left. Other friends brought meals, helped make arrangements for my older kids to come home, sent notes of encouragement, texted me with prayers, and just showed up on my doorstep to do whatever needed to be done.

We all hope that crisis never hits our family, but life is hard and sometimes the unexpected happens. Death, divorce, illness, infidelity, cancer—we hope those words aren't ever used to describe our circumstances, but there's no way to be insulated from them touching us in some way. When—not if—they do, we need to have friends who will help carry the load for us.

How is your friendship bank? Is it time to make some investments? Life has its ups and downs, and we need each other through both. Friendship requires an investment of time and energy. Today is the day for you to call a friend you want to get to know better or invest in a friendship you already have. Set up coffee, arrange a girls' night out, do something to get some money in your friendship bank. You never know when you'll need to make a withdrawal.

APPLY THE ANTIDOTE

You can do all the right things, and you'll still come face-to-face with imperfect friends. That's because we're all human, and no one is perfect. Of course, you're not perfect either, so it's likely there will be times you will frustrate your friends, too! What do we do when expectation does not meet reality? How can we keep the Perfection Infection at bay when it comes to navigating friendships? Here are some practical strategies:

Change Your Expectations

Are you catching on yet? We're not lowering our expectations; we're changing them to better match reality. Friends are an important part of life. Not every mom you meet will become a good friend. Good friends are imperfect, and they will mess up, not handle a situation the way you wanted them to handle it, and forget to text you back or return a call on occasion. If you expect imperfection, you won't be disappointed when it shows up. You'll also be a more grace-filled, loving friend, if you set your expectations to better track with reality.

Pursue Humility

Humility happens when we are wrong, admit it, and ask for forgiveness. Being a humble friend allows us to admit our mistakes, clean them up, and resist being defined by them.

If we are prone to compare our insides to someone else's outsides, it's likely we'll do that with our friends, too. It's easy to jump to conclusions about someone else, thinking they are either better or worse than we are. It's uncomfortable to acknowledge, but if we pay attention to our thought life, pride happens more often than we like to admit. When that little voice whispers in our heads, "If she would only _____, then her child would _____." "If she would only _____, then her husband would _____." When we have the answer for other people, that's pride. Humility says, "I don't know the answer, but I feel your pain." It also says, "I don't struggle with _____, but I sure do struggle with _____." Pride says, "I have the answers you need." Humility says, "I still have a lot to learn. I don't know it all."

Pursue Courage

Fear will keep issues unaddressed in a friendship. It takes courage to have honest conversation when things need to be talked about in a friendship. Learn to "ask your thoughts." If you felt uncomfortable with something a friend said, ask her about it. If you feel distance in your relationship, ask about it by saying something like, "Are we okay?" I recently had a meeting with several people at my publishing house. After the meeting, my editor sent me an email, saying, "I thought that the time we spent together talking about the [book] was a little strained. Perhaps I was imagining it, but if there is anything you would like to talk about, just give me a call." I was so glad she stated her thoughts. I responded to her that I didn't feel that way at all and was personally okay. She then responded with a thank you for the reassurance. That's what courage looks like!

Be Confident

Insecurity says we aren't worth someone's time and energy, but confidence says we are valuable and have something to offer to a friendship. Confidence comes from defining ourselves as God sees us: forgiven, loved, valuable, and filled with hope and promise. We're not perfect, but we are in the process of being perfected. In other words, God wants us to become more like Christ each and every day. Carry your God-fidence with you when you reach out to meet someone. Carry your God-fidence with you when you need to have an honest conversation with a friend. Carry your God-fidence with you when life throws a curve and a friend disappoints you. Confidence gives us strength to stare down the Perfection Infection and put it in its place.

....

While moms are usually the teachers of manners, they also need to "mind their manners" when interacting with other moms. Though I've never seen an etiquette book on mothering, there are general courtesies moms can give to one another that make up the "Mommy Manners." When I sat down with a group of moms to discuss this topic, these are the manners we found important:

❧ When visiting someone's house with children in tow, before you leave always help put away toys the children played with. This models responsibility for your children and shows respect to the hostess.

❧ If you are in a quiet, public setting (such as a meeting or church service) with an infant or small child and the child fusses or cries, always step out of the room to settle the child the minute he or she starts fussing. This is respectful to those around you who are trying to hear the speaker or maintain focus.

❧ If your baby or toddler has a dirty diaper while you are visiting someone's home, never put the stinky diaper in that family's trash can. Most moms agree that you have two options: 1) Keep plastic bags in your diaper bag for carrying the diaper back to your home to throw away, or 2) Ask for the location of their outdoor trash can so you can dispose of the diaper outside the house or building.

❧ After someone has a baby, give her a call when you are at the store and offer to pick up milk, bread, or whatever her family might need.

❧ Always RSVP promptly to invitations your children receive.

❧ Offer to pay for gas when sharing a ride to your children's out-of-town sporting event.

❧ Offer to hold the door open for a mom entering a store with a stroller. If you're not a stroller-pushing mom anymore, remember that was you once!

❧ Be the first to wave while walking or driving down your street.

❖ Offer to take your neighbor's children if you're going to the same event, lesson, or camp.

❖ When your children have had a friend spend the night, have the visiting child's sleepover bags packed, sleeping bag ready, and shoes by the door at the predetermined time the parents will be arriving for pickup.

❖ When going to someone's house for a luncheon play date, offer to bring your own lunches or snacks. This can take the burden off the hostess mom and eliminates picky eater syndrome. She may refuse, but at least you offered!

❖ Remember to respect another mom's way of doing things even if it is different from the way you do it!

❖ Be a good listener. Don't try to top another mom's story; just allow her to share her story. If she's frustrated, allow her to vent! Just knowing someone listened and cared makes such a difference.

Here's one more: If you have two children close in age and one gets an invitation to do something special (play at a friend's house, go to a birthday party, etc.), do not assume that your other child can just go along. I recently heard about a mom who dropped off her four-year-old son at a birthday party. As she was leaving, her three-year-old son began to throw a temper tantrum because he couldn't stay so she asked the host mom if it would be okay for the sibling to stay, too. Don't even think about it, Mom! Our kids need to know they don't always get to do the things their siblings get to do and their siblings don't get to do everything they get to do.

Courteous, thoughtful moms usually raise courteous, helpful kids because, with kids, more is caught than taught. As you interact with other moms, make sure you mind your mommy manners because little eyes are watching!

Be Grace-Filled

When we are dealing with imperfect people, judgment can really creep into our hearts. We can internally point the finger at someone else rather than pay attention to the three fingers pointing back at us. Grace happens when we allow another person to be human. It is found by a quick act of forgiveness on our part when someone lets us down. If we intentionally root out judgment in our hearts, we will, one mom at a time, start to end the mommy wars. No more stay-at-home mom against the working mom. No more breast-feeding moms vs. bottle-feeding moms. Love will reign, grace will prevail, and we can learn to encourage one another even as we make different choices in our personal lives.

Talk to God

God doesn't ask us to do anything He wasn't willing to do Himself. Jesus lived life with His friends who are referred to as the "disciples" in the Bible. He also had His friends Mary, Martha, and Lazarus. He spent time with them, challenged them, encouraged them, ate with them, laughed with them, and got frustrated with them. In fact, Jesus' friends let Him down in the garden of Gethsemane. He asked them to pray with Him as He was dealing with the emotions of facing an imminent death on the cross. His friends told Him they would pray, but they fell asleep instead (you can read the story in Matthew 26:36–45). Can you imagine the disappointment Jesus must have felt? Any challenges you are facing with friendship you can talk to God about because He experienced them, too! We have a friend who understands!

EMBRACE YOUR BEAUTIFUL, IMPERFECT FRIENDS

Have you ever thought about what your life would have been like without one of your friends? Even if this is a "sparse" friendship season for you, can you identify some women who have influenced your life and encouraged you in some way? Take a minute and write one friend a note of thanks today. Tell her what you appreciate about her and what she has brought to your life.

There are no perfect friends — just fellow moms, trying to do their best and discovering that there's more joy in doing life together.

CHAPTER 7

NO MORE *Perfect* DAYS

The day I started to write this chapter, my fifteen-year-old son had spent the night at a friend's house. My husband was camping with friends, and my older son was working, so I was enjoying a Saturday morning home alone.

There were a ton of garage sales in a neighborhood just down the street so I called my walking friend, Crystal, and asked her if she wanted to multitask—walk and garage sale at the same time! I headed down to the neighborhood and had just stopped at my first garage sale when my phone rang. It was my fifteen-year-old. "Mom, we got up early this morning and went disc golfing. We're finished. Can you come and get me?" When I asked him where he was, he said he was at the course on the other side of town. It wasn't just around the corner, so I could push

Motherhood is the ministry of availability.

the pause button and run to get him. Since I was the only POD (parent on duty), I had no choice but to throw out my plans and do what I needed to do.

Ahhh, the joy of motherhood. There are no perfect days.

I like to say that motherhood is the ministry of availability. You could also say it's the ministry of interruptions! Let's face it: Life with kids is unpredictable. Their propensity to live "in the moment" clashes easily with our "perfect plans." In fact, when I called my friend Crystal to see if she wanted to walk and garage sale, she was at the store with her four-year-old (just one of her six kids!). She said she'd join me when she got home. An hour later she called and said, "This is taking a lot longer than I anticipated. We've made several trips to the bathroom, and my four-year-old's needs are taking a priority over the grocery shopping. I don't think I'll make it before the garage sales close." So her perfect plans went right out the window, too!

Learning to live with kids requires making major adjustments in our realistic expectations. We have to learn to expect the unexpected, find flexibility, and increase the margin. Instead of getting frustrated, let's stop expecting a fantasy and instead embrace reality.

EXPECT THE UNEXPECTED

After my garage sale/walking plans went out the window, I headed home to work on this chapter. With absolutely nothing on the calendar, I had set aside the day for writing. I'd been writing about an hour when my son flopped on the couch exasperated. He was leading worship at church the next day and had been in the living room alternately playing guitar and piano and trying to select what songs we would be singing. Carrying the responsibility for leading always produces a lot of anxiety for him. Our worship director at church saw the potential for leadership in Austin and was mentoring him as a worship leader. He occasionally gave him the opportunity to be the sole leader on Sunday morning. What a great learning opportunity this was—but, oh, the blood, sweat, and tears that it always produced.

However, we'd been here before. I knew that planning the worship music and the transitions between songs would cause a lot of stress in my man-boy. So I laid aside my computer, joined him on the couch, and helped him sort through his feelings for about a half hour. "Help son deal with emotions" wasn't on my to-do list. Things like that never are. However, I knew this issue could pop up at some point in time before Sunday. I couldn't plan for it exactly, but I could anticipate its occurrence.

That's what "expecting the unexpected" looks like. It's anticipating that your newborn will fill not only his diaper, but his onesie as well, just as you're walking out the door to go to church. It's expecting your two-year-old to fall and scrape her knee while you're making dinner. It's expecting your five-year-old to ask twenty-five questions when you've only got the patience for two. It's anticipating that your junior-high daughter will call and want to spend the night at her friend's house after she's been there all afternoon. It's expecting your teenager to need some love, reassurance, and face-to-face conversation as a decision or situation suddenly becomes overwhelming.

People need time. Caring takes time. Conversations require time. These are the real, but often unanticipated, elements of real life. Interruptions—aka real life—are the work of motherhood. There's no way around it. It is what it is. Why then do the interruptions throw us off so often?

It all comes down to control. There's absolutely no way to control real life — and that doesn't settle well for most of us. We want to be in control. We want life to go the way we want. We make a plan, and we errantly expect it to come to fruition. When it doesn't go the way we planned, we find ourselves angry, frustrated, and grasping to maintain the illusion of control.

In her book *Let. It. Go.: How to Stop Running the Show and Start Walking in Faith*, Karen Ehman addresses imperfect days.

> Our best-laid plans don't always come to fruition. Weekly, if not daily, we face delays, interruptions, sidetracking issues, and inconveniences. They may come by way of the phone, an email, or a knock on the door.
>
> Someone has a crisis. So they summon you. And now? Well, their crisis is suddenly now your crisis, too.
>
> Or you are thrown a last-minute loop in the form of a sick child who needs caring for or a hurting neighbor who could use a listening ear. Or the washing machine decides to give up the ghost, sending you across town to the Laundromat. So you must pause. Rearrange. Even opt out of your self-scripted agenda altogether. Yes, ma'am. This unplanned side trip has you steaming.
>
> It isn't always a major interruption in your day that causes you grief. The minor hiccups can be just as disheartening. A child has a question that pulls us away from the task we are tackling. Juice gets spilled or soup is slopped, requiring your attention. A family member on a different floor needs Mom (no, Dad will not do),

....

and it detours you and threatens to arrest your progress.

If, by chance, your best-laid plans get interrupted or derailed, how do you respond? Do we choose at such delicate junctures to exert the helpful, needful control you *should* seek—that of our tongue? Or do we let it hurl and unfurl, taking out loved ones in its path?[1]

Control is really a mirage.

Control is really a mirage. The only control you and I can really have is self-control, and the Bible says that is a fruit of the Spirit. In other words, we can't have self-control on our own; it comes from letting God be the real leader of our lives and the manager of our hearts.

As Karen reminds us, we can plan, but when our plans go awry, we need self-control to hold our tongues. We can set goals, but when something blocks our goals, we need self-control to keep anger at bay. We can think through the details of a project, but when it doesn't go as planned, we need the self-control to roll with the changes that become necessary.

More importantly, we need perspective to keep us from reacting when our plans fall through. We need the perspective that the moment we are in is just as important as the moment we planned on that didn't happen the way we thought it would. Think about that for a moment. Underline it or highlight it if you can. We need to embrace "what is" instead of "what could have been." This is so valuable to understand because if you and I could learn that the moment we are in is just as important as the moment we planned, we could completely change the way we interact with our families.

When we don't value the moment we are in as much as the one we planned, we'll miss out on precious time with those we love. Sometimes

....

we'll do more than miss out on precious time with them, we'll ruin an unexpected opportunity given to us.

On one such day when my son Evan was fifteen, he and I had made a three-hour drive to spend the day with my parents. Evan had his driver's permit and asked to drive the entire three-hour journey home. I was happy to oblige. About forty-five minutes from home, the car began to sputter and completely died on the side of the road. As I assessed what the problem was, I quickly realized we'd run out of gas. Evan was flabbergasted. He couldn't believe he had not paid attention to the gas tank. Immediately a battle began in my mind between being angry about the situation he'd put us in or giving him grace because, after all, we all make mistakes.

It was below zero outside, and there was no exit within sight. A call for a tow truck indicated it would take about an hour for help to arrive. The battle continued in my mind until I finally resolved in my heart that my anger would do no good. I chose to proceed with love and grace. And then I had the most precious hour with my fifteen-year-old son. We talked. We laughed. We talked some more. The moment we were in was not a moment I had planned at all. In fact, we were in a pickle. However, because I kept perspective in this spontaneous moment, we turned it into a beautiful opportunity for connection. It's one of my most precious memories of time spent with my son during his teen years.

When we expect the unexpected, we prepare our hearts to handle whatever comes our way. If our hearts are soft and flexible, we will more likely respond with love rather than frustration.

FIND FLEXIBILITY

Why is it we believe that the way we plan things is the right way—or even the only way? Let's say it's a Saturday afternoon. You've fed your kids and you're getting ready to put your two-year-old down for her nap. The usual nap routine is to finish lunch, read two books, and then put her in her crib to sleep. Today she wants to go outside and see the butterflies. Why not be flexible? How about five minutes of butterflies and then five minutes of reading?

Or you're planning on a night out with your husband, but he comes home with a splitting headache. He asks if plans could be changed to stay home, order in, and watch a movie. Couldn't an evening home with your husband be just as valuable as a night out?

It's a Tuesday afternoon. You plan to take your teen out for a Coke tonight. As you're preparing dinner, she opens up about her struggles with a friendship at school. It's not the best time for the discussion. It would be better to wait until just the two of you are out later. But teenagers are emotional beings; you can't "schedule" important conversations. So why not now? Why can't you push the pause button on dinner prep to tend to the heart of your daughter?

Yes, there's the practical side to each of these scenarios. Your two-year-old thrives on routine and you don't want to mess that up. However, will a slight change in the routine really throw the whole routine out the window? Not going out on a date changes the dynamics of your time together, but you can still be together, can't you? And yes, there are usually other people in the house who are hungry and looking forward to dinner. But what if it was part of your family's DNA that people always take priority over tasks? Would the others understand?

....

Most of us didn't grow up in an environment with that much flexibility and sensitivity to others. We don't have any model for this kind of mindset unless we look at the life of Jesus Christ. When Jesus lived on this earth, He set the example for how to live out the ministry of interruption.

In my book *Real Moms . . . Real Jesus*, I take a look at the human experience of Jesus. Many of His human experiences are like ours as moms, and handling interruptions was part of that. There's the time when Jesus was on His way from Judea to Galilee. The trip took Him through a city called Samaria, where He met a woman at the well when He stopped to get a drink and rest from His trip. Jesus was headed to Galilee with a purpose in mind, but His journey was interrupted by this interaction with a Samaritan woman. The narrative says that Jesus was worn out from the trip, yet He embraced this opportunity and engaged in a life-changing conversation with this woman.

There is another story in the Bible about a time when Jesus went through Jericho on His way to Jerusalem. There was a tax collector named Zacchaeus who wanted so badly to see Jesus that He climbed a tree to catch a glimpse of Him. Jesus saw Zacchaeus and told him that they needed to spend time together. Jesus had a plan in place, but when life happened, He adjusted.

Ministry for Jesus was the person standing in front of Him, regardless of whether that interaction was planned or spontaneous. We can learn from Jesus' examples. Ministry for us is the person standing in front of us — even if we weren't expecting things to happen the way they are playing out.

My flexibility has increased the more I've learned to let God lead my life. In fact, I've come to see many of these not-planned-for moments not as interruptions but rather as God's appointments. They are moments I didn't plan for, but God did.

On my second day of writing this chapter, I had plans for lunch after church, but my husband, who had been camping with a couple of guy friends about fifteen miles from our house, asked me to join him at the campsite for lunch. My two teens had already asked if they could each go home with a friend. It wasn't my plan at all to go to the campground; in fact, it wasn't even on the radar screen and I was hardly dressed for it. However, after changing my plans and joining him for lunch at the campsite, I could see why it was God's plan. I was able to "step into his world" for a bit, allowing us to connect in a way that was important to him. I was able to visit with his friend who was still at the campsite. The three of us enjoyed a leisurely lunch and relaxed conversation. My husband later thanked me for changing plans and coming out to the campsite.

When it comes to adjusting plans, how flexible are you? I wish I could say I'm characterized by flexibility. I'm more easygoing than I used to be, but I'm still working on this in my own life. Some personalities lend themselves to this more than others. A creative, spontaneous mom finds flexibility much easier than a type A, get-it-done mom who likes her ducks in a row. Regardless of your personality, however, the ability to be flexible has a direct correlation to how many activities are crammed into your day. Just how much can one mom really do?

EMBRACE THE SPACE

I stumbled upon her blog one afternoon and I knew immediately that we were kindred spirits. Rachel is known as the "Hands Free Mama" at www.handsfreemama.com. She's a mom who's learned to embrace the space so she can love her real life. In this excerpt from my blog interview with Rachel, you can see how she has intentionally created space for real life to happen in her home.

What launched your "Hands Free" journey?

Almost two years ago, I experienced what I call my "break-down-breakthrough." For the first time, I honestly answered the complimentary question I received on a daily basis: "How do you do it all?"

I painfully admitted that I was able to "do it all" because I missed out on life—the playing, connecting, memory-making parts of life. With clarity, I saw the damage that a massive to-do list, a constantly buzzing phone, and an overscheduled calendar was having on my relationships, my health, and my life.

Once I acknowledged that living distracted is not really living at all, I vowed to change. I began taking small steps to let go of distraction by creating designated times of the day to be *fully* present with the people I love.

Where do you see moms struggling with distraction?

There are two types of distraction in society today that prevent many moms from grasping "the moments that matter." One type is *external distraction*, which includes technology, electronic devices, overcommitted schedules, and excessive to-do lists. The other type is *internal distraction*, which includes pressure to be perfect, comparing ourselves to others, feelings of guilt, shame, and inadequacy, just to name a few.

What have you "downsized" that you thought you'd miss, but you really haven't?

I started my "Hands Free" journey by letting go of some of the small, immediate distractions and then moved on to the larger activities and commitments that sabotaged my time, focus, energy, and joy. I created a life mission statement by asking myself: What are the most important things I must do in my lifetime? From the short list of "must dos" I created, I was able to better decide what activities and commitments to say YES to and which ones to decline.

Over the past two years I have drastically scaled back my extracurricular commitments and social activities. I have also scaled down my circle of friends to consist of a small core group of women who share similar values and a quest for authenticity. Now I can honestly say that everything I say yes to is something I find value in or feel passionate about. I am no longer resentful and depleted by having "too much on my plate."

What have you gained in your "Hands Free" journey?

I have gained uncountable "moments that matter"—moments that would have been tragically missed had I continued living distracted. In these precious moments, I have gained the ability to know my children and my spouse. I know every good and precious thing about each of them because we spend time together talking and interacting. I have also come to know and accept myself. I know my faults and my weaknesses, but I also know my strengths and my gifts.

How would you encourage a mom to begin her own "Hands Free" journey?

My journey began with one small step of letting go of my distractions to cuddle with my child on the couch. That first step can be as simple as closing your laptop, turning away from the laundry and the dishes, shutting off the phone, or sticking the to-do list in a drawer. Simply let go of your distractions and immerse yourself in what (or who) really matters to you.

Watch her breath, listen to his words, memorize her face. In those beautiful moments of connection, time has a way of standing still; the insignificant falls away. Whether you "let go" for ten minutes or two hours, you will feel an overwhelming sense of peace and connection you cannot find when you are distracted. Immediately, you will yearn to experience that meaningful connection again and again until it becomes the practice of your life.

Once you see what you have been missing, you don't want to go back to the way it was before. By living "Hands Free," your eyes will be opened to what really matters and a meaningful life will be within your grasp.[2]

Rachel has learned about something called "margin." She's experienced what it's like to function as a mom with lots of distractions. Now she's embracing a life with minimal distractions.

Have you ever given thought to the importance of the white space on a book's page? Because of the white space in between the lines, you're able to read the black words. Because of the margins at the top, bottom, and sides, the words are formatted for an easy read. We don't often think about the margin, but if it were missing and all the words

....

jumbled together on a page, we'd immediately notice its absence.

After reading the book *Margin* by Dr. Richard Swenson (NavPress), I learned margin is important in more than just newspapers, school reports, and published books. Our lives need margin to find the balance we all long for. Whether we realize it or not, our bodies, our relationships, and even our finances need white space to function at their best. Most importantly for an imperfect mom living out her imperfect days, margin is essential in handling the twists and turns of everyday family life.

What does margin look like in real life? Margin is having the pace and space in your day to allow real life to happen. Too many of us run at a pace that is not only unhealthy physically but damaging relationally. We go-go-go, telling ourselves there are just not enough hours in the day, when we really need to be slowing down and enjoying the journey just as much as we anticipate enjoying the destination when we arrive.

When we cram too much into our schedules or our kids' schedules, we aren't leaving sufficient white space for the ebb and flow of human experiences. Plans change, emotions rise, children cry, heads ache, keys get lost, recipes flop, conversations start, and weather happens. That's life—real life. In order to expect the unexpected and maintain flexibility, we have to have enough time built into our schedules to anticipate what will likely happen.

I'm working on this when it comes to being punctual. I've never been much of a clock-watcher. While it doesn't matter when I'm the only person affected by my late arrival, it does matter when others are affected by my lateness. So I'm paying attention to the realistic margin I need to get out the door. I've come to realize that I consistently underestimate the time needed to accomplish the tasks I need to do before

. . . .

walking out the door. Without fail, I also misjudge the number of tasks I need to do before I leave. When the kids were little, I'd remember just as I was walking out the door that I hadn't restocked the diaper bag. Even now as a mom of teens, I get ready to walk out the door only to remember a permission slip I needed to sign or a check I needed to send to school with one of my boys. Invariably, I grab my keys and my purse to be gone for the day only to remember that I was going to put a roast in the Crock-Pot for dinner. Whether it's misjudging my time or what I need to accomplish within that time, not having enough margin puts unnecessary stress on me and my family.

So, how do we increase margin and decrease distractions so we can more appropriately handle our imperfect days? We can choose to implement some of these "margin minders" to increase the white space in our lives:

Trust Experience

We all have the tendency to think unrealistically. We'll tell ourselves, "It only takes me ten minutes to drive to church. Since church starts at 10:00, we'll leave at 9:45. That will give us five minutes to spare." Experience says that when you've left at 9:45 in the past, you've been late nine times out of ten because you haven't expected the unexpected. No matter how much you rationalize it in your mind, experience wins over your internal logic. Adjust your time to leave based upon realistic experience.

Set Boundaries

Boundaries are healthy for us and for our kids. It's okay to set boundaries for yourself, such as, "I won't be gone more than one night a week for volunteer or church activities." It's also okay to set boundaries for your kids like, "We won't overlap sports. You'll have to choose which one you like best." I have a personal commitment not to attend home parties (i.e., Pampered Chef, Thirty-One, etc.). Some people love them. Personally, I don't have the time or the money, so I just don't do them—at all. This boundary also helps me keep margin because it seems I'm invited to several each month.

Say No

There's no way to keep healthy white space in our lives unless we learn to say no. We can't do everything. We can't please everyone. Even Jesus knew when it was time to say no and stop teaching or healing because he was weary. I've learned never to say yes on the spot. I take twenty-four hours to think, pray, and talk with my husband before saying yes. I've also learned there are gracious ways to say no. Try something like, "Thank you for thinking of me. I won't be able to help out/join you/ attend this time." Often, no other explanation is needed.

Increase Time

When children are involved, every activity will take longer than you anticipate. Increase the time you set aside to make dinner, since you will be interrupted several times. Increase the time you set aside to go to the grocery store; the little ones will need to go potty, probably more than once. Increase the time you think it will take you to complete a project; things never go as planned, and someone will need your attention in the midst of it.

Decrease Activities

Put less into your day. Children's needs take time. Relationships take time. Conversations take time. While none of us puts those kinds of things on our "to do" list, they are an important part of our day. My friend Kelly tells herself to "embrace the space." This is her way of remembering the time requirements of human relationships and putting breathing space into her daily schedule.

We need margin in other areas of our lives, too. For instance, we need margin in our finances. Is there more month than money? Up to your eyeballs in debt? Living paycheck to paycheck? If your answer is "yes" to any of the above, it's probably time to increase your financial margin. Save for the future. Expect the unexpected by putting money away to pay for them when they happen. Resist the urge to spend every penny you have. If there's no financial margin, it will definitely exacerbate the Perfection Infection in your life. When the car breaks down, and there's no money in savings to fix it, you'll find your stress meter off the charts. When your child gets sick and needs an expensive prescription, you'll find yourself overwhelmed with the financial implications. Cars break down, and kids get sick; that's reality. Let's expect those things, plan for them, and put the financial margin in place to handle them when they come along.

Relationships take energy.

We also need margin in emotional energy. Relationships take energy. If we are emotionally depleted, we risk not having the energy to successfully navigate a marital disagreement or a difficult parenting issue. When emotional margin is present we increase compassion and empathy and decrease apathy. Rest, laugh, and focus on "being" and not "doing" to increase much-needed emotional margin.

Finally, physical margin is extremely important. How much sleep are you getting? Are you eating healthy foods? Exercising regularly? Our bodies need rest, good nutrition, and regular exercise to function well. Go to bed just a little earlier, reduce your sugar intake, and choose the steps over the elevator in an effort to increase physical margin. This will give you the physical fuel to function at your very best.

The by-product of a margin-less life is stress. A life with margin discovers the beauty of contentment, simplicity, balance, and rest. That was enough motivation for me to make some lifestyle changes that have deepened my relationships, improved my health, decreased my stress, and helped me navigate the reality of my imperfect days.

BEWARE THE COMPARE

It's easy to look at other moms and assume their days go better than ours do. We're hard on ourselves because we are most familiar with our weaknesses. When we're critical of ourselves, we can easily make false assumptions about other moms and how they handle their days. That's why our honesty is important for the moms we interact with.

Molly sums this up well in an email she sent me after reading through my blog, "Thanks for keeping it real. So often, I see the pictures of big, happy families and think, 'Gosh, I bet she never scrapes crusted food off her clothes, or rinses snot from the sick wee one out of her hair.' Amazing how pictures can look perfect, but then in reality, life happens to everyone . . . super messy homes, crusty/snotty mom, sick kids, and other struggles."

When we keep it real, we help other moms know they are normal. Not only that, but when we verbalize our struggles, we remind ourselves that we're normal, too. Camaraderie is made up of understanding, understanding comes from revelation, and revelation starts with honesty. Resist the urge to compare and determine you come up short. There are no perfect moms living out perfect days, but there are all kinds of imperfect moms handling whatever life throws our way the absolute best way we can!

APPLY THE ANTIDOTE

Of course changing expectations is what this chapter has been about. When we have unrealistic expectations of how the day will go, we set ourselves—and our husbands and children—up for failure. There's nothing worse for a husband than to be constantly disappointing his wife because he doesn't measure up to what she expects. There's nothing worse for a child than to always be letting down his mother. If we don't realize that unrealistic expectations are present, we'll unknowingly put hairline fractures in the foundation of the most important relationships in our lives.

All four of our antidotes pertain to dealing with imperfect days in some way, but there are two to explore more deeply here. Let's help ourselves and those we love handle real life in the best way possible with these transitions.

Turn from Pride and Embrace Humility

Pride keeps the real stuff hidden so we appear better than we really are. Pride keeps our mask in place. It doesn't help us, and it doesn't help other moms.

Pride also demands. It controls. Too often pride says, "I've got it together. Now don't get in my way." That's what happens when we pridefully push through our jam-packed day. If just one person gets in our way and upsets our tightly wound schedule, pride condemns whatever or whoever got in the way.

Conversely, humility is concerned more about the people than the project. Humility cares. Humility bends. Most often humility says, "Well, this wasn't the way I planned it, but I trust that God's in charge and I am not." Humility has nothing to protect—not a schedule or a reputation—because it realizes that God is in control and He is the one who determines our value.

Here are three practical ways to turn from pride and embrace humility when handling an imperfect day:

Pay attention to how much you want to control. Recognize that control is really about pride and a lack of trust. Tell God you are sorry that you don't trust Him to have your best at heart. Ask Him to help you learn to trust His plans more than your plans. Thank Him for His forgiveness and grace when you blow it.

Keep it real. If you're on Facebook, post an honest status about something that didn't go the way you planned. Don't pretty it up. Just be honest. Then ask if anyone can relate. You will not only be reminded that you're not alone, you'll help one of your friends know she's not alone in her struggles.

Ask God for help. One mom said the best advice her mom ever gave her was to get up in the morning and give your day to God. Tell Him, "Here's what I planned. Help me to deal graciously with however it *really* turns out."

. . . .

Transition from Judgment to Grace

Judgment lashes out and blames when things don't go as planned. Grace sees the big picture. It allows others to be human and expects life to be real. Judgment looks at others and comes to conclusions about them, even without having full information. Grace looks at others and simply sees broken people trying to do their best. Judgment says my plan, my way, and my efforts are the best. Grace says my plan, my way, and my efforts are just one option in accomplishing this goal.

Here are two strategies you can use to move from judgment to grace:

Be honest with yourself. It's so much easier to see shortcomings in other people's lives than it is to see them in our own hearts. When we judge, we build a wall between us and someone else — and we're the only one laying the bricks! God tells us that it's His job to judge, not ours. Watch where you unconsciously look at others and judge their lives, actions, or intent without them even knowing it. This will help you move out of the trap of comparing your insides to other people's outsides and finding yourself feeling "less than."

Think about these questions and answer them honestly:

+ What if I occasionally resisted the urge to plan, and instead enjoyed whatever happened?
+ What if I stopped looking at the future and learned to live in the moment instead?
+ What if I lived out my values but resisted measuring life by specific expected outcomes?

✦ What if I stopped trying to control others and focused instead on being kind to them?

   ✦ What if I learned to accept the world as it is, rather than being frustrated with it, stressed by it, mad at it, or trying to change it into what I want it to be?

   ✦ What if I was never disappointed with how things turn out because I never expected anything specific?

   ✦ What if I could just accept what happens?

EMBRACE YOUR BEAUTIFUL, IMPERFECT DAY

Have you had any God appointments today? Can you watch for moments when you have the opportunity to successfully embrace "what is" and let go of "what is not"? Ask God to give you a heart of joy that appreciates whatever moment you are experiencing—even if it wasn't something you planned.

There are no perfect days—just precious moments you and I are offered to practice the ministry of availability.

Notes

1. Karen Ehman, *Let. It. Go.: How to Stop Running the Show and Start Walking in Faith* (Grand Rapids: Zondervan, 2012), 136–37.
2. Author interview with Rachel Macy Stafford, "Meet the 'Hands-Free Mama,'" Jill Savage blog, May 8, 2012, www.jillsavage.org.

CHAPTER 8

NO MORE *Perfect* HOMES

*D*uring the 2007 Hearts at Home conference, I started my keynote message with a video tour of my house. We filmed the video on a "normal" day at the Savage household. I purposely didn't straighten the house or clean things up. I led the viewer from the side door into the kitchen—even opening the refrigerator door to see the disorganized condition of my fridge. There were piles of papers on my desk and folded laundry covering my bed. This three-minute video tour was so powerful that I fully believe I could have walked off the stage and said

> *We are on a journey to make peace with real life.*

no more, and the message would have been just as effective. In fact, recently a mom watched the video on my blog and left this comment, "I am promising myself to make peace with the way our home is, and will be, with five of us living in it." I love her choice of words: *make peace*. We are on a journey to make peace with real life, aren't we?

We've all seen enough television shows, movies, and magazine layouts that we consciously and unconsciously compare our living environments with picture-perfect photos we see in our heads. Kids create clutter, and it's time for us to understand that mess is part of the territory. Sure, some moms have better organizational skills than others, but the truth is we all need a more accurate picture in our mind of what a "normal" home with kids will look like.

Of course, each season of motherhood is unique. Kid clutter comprises different kinds of toys and "stuff" depending on the age of your children. In the infant years, kid clutter is made up of rattles, plastic books, and bright-colored toys of all shapes and sizes. The preschool years are filled with simple puzzles, cardboard books, and interactive toys that teach shapes, numbers, and colors. If there's one word to describe the grade school years, it is "pieces." There are hundreds of pieces: puzzle pieces, Lego parts, Barbie doll shoes, and dozens of other creative parts you're sure to discover when walking barefoot in the dark! Then, you enter the late grade school, preteen, and teen years: sports gear, music books, socks, empty potato chip bags, iPods, ear buds, and other "stuff" you're forever asking them to pick up and put away.

Let's take a stroll through the average home to get a picture of what real life looks like. As we take our home "tour," we'll establish a picture of "normal" for each room so we can all relax and realize that our homes and families are normal. We'll also learn some tips and strategies we can use to help manage the imperfect home we live in!

KITCHEN

The kitchen is the heartbeat of the home. It's where we spend a large majority of our time with friends and family. It's where we have wonderful, impromptu family conversations. It's where food and fellowship are shared with friends and neighbors—whether the gatherings are planned or spontaneous. It's also where everybody tends to dump whatever is in their hands when they walk in the door!

Every one of us struggles with the same clutter issues in the kitchen: kitchen gadgets, countertop appliances, dirty dishes, school papers, mail, keys, permission slips, appointment reminders, recipes (and I created this list simply by sitting at my kitchen island and documenting everything cluttering my kitchen counters). I asked my Facebook and blog friends what was currently sitting on their kitchen counters and more than a hundred moms responded within minutes! Some of the things they added were last night's dishes from dinner, groceries yet to be put away, trash needing to be thrown away, and dishes soaking. Then there were the really honest responses of some unique things sitting on kitchen counters like thousands of pop tabs in containers, an athletic supporter, chicken feed and antibiotics, a hot glue gun, two baby sparrows (really??), shoes and dirty socks, and an unidentified sticky substance.

My favorite response, however, was this one: A mom reported that she had a hundred praying mantises hatching from an egg sack on her counter. She said her child had carried the egg sack in from the outside and set it on the counter, and in no time they began to hatch!

Now do you feel better about what's sitting on your kitchen counter? We all struggle to keep this room under control. Keeping our

....

kitchens uncluttered is like shoveling snow while it's still snowing! So what's a mom to do?

The first objective is to change our expectations. It's unlikely that our kitchens will look like any magazine picture we'll ever see! Real people do not live in the magazine pictures, and even when it's a photo of a real person's kitchen, the picture is staged by designers and photographers, not snapped in the midst of real family living. A healthy goal is enough organization so that you can find things easily, enough cleanliness and counter space so you can make a meal, and enough convenience that you can access the things you need on a regular basis. Wanting your kitchen to look perfect will most assuredly turn you into the Mommy Monster, and no one likes to be around when the Mommy Monster shows up!

If you struggle with keeping the kitchen under control (not perfect—just functional!), here are some tried and true tips:

Evaluate your clutter. Categorize the things that are cluttering your kitchen counters. Usually you'll find broad categories like mail, school papers, keys, bills, coupons, etc. Create a "home" for each broad category. A countertop hanging file box with labeled files or a horizontal desktop organizer may be just what you need.

Get in the habit of putting things in their new "home." Take your husband and kids on a "field trip" in the kitchen, explaining to them where they are now to put school papers, mail, keys, etc. Retrain yourself to put things in their new place, too.

Open mail by the trash can or recycling bin. Throw away envelopes and junk mail right away, and put bills and other papers in their appointed place.

Clear countertop papers daily. This helps you keep chaos under control.

Put as many kitchen appliances away as you can. If you don't use your toaster or blender every day and you have cabinet space to spare, store them out of sight.

The kitchen is the place where the family lives. Be realistic about your expectations, even if you decide to put new organizational strategies into place. Remember any organizational strategy will always be challenged by the stuff of real family life.

BATHROOM

Just like the kitchen, the bathroom gets a lot of abuse. At one time in the Savage household, our main bathroom was shared by six of us. That's a lot of toothbrushes, hairbrushes, deodorants, and bobby pins!

Like the counter in the kitchen, the bathroom counter also seems to be a landing place for personal items: toothpaste, contact solution, mouthwash, cotton balls, Q-tips, dental floss, medicine, hair barrettes, and ponytail holders. Depending on your season of motherhood, you might add in bath toys, diapers, diaper rash cream, and hooded towels.

Bathrooms are lived in strenuously. They get a lot of use, especially when it's shower and bath time. While we'd love for them to be picture-perfect, a realistic expectation is that they be regularly cleaned and organized enough so family members can find what they need.

*H*ere are some tried and true tips for conquering bathroom maintenance from moms in the trenches:

Use drawer organizers in bathroom drawers to keep all the miscellaneous items in a place you can find them.

If you don't have enough drawer space, **use countertop baskets** to organize things like bobby pins, barrettes, and pony-tail holders.

Keep cleaning supplies in each bathroom for quick sink and counter wipes.

Pick one day a week to clean the toilets, bathtub, shower, counters, and floor. This is one room of the house that you can't let go too long!

Give yourself and your family some grace when it comes to the bathroom. So what if you are the only one who seems to know how to put toilet paper on the dispenser? So what if the bathroom looks like a tornado hit after bath time? Look around, smile, and thank God for your messy family!

BEDROOMS

I asked my Facebook friends what the oddest/grossest thing they've found in their child's bedroom was. Oh, my! You just wouldn't believe what they shared! Here are some of the responses: row of many boogers wiped along the wall; rotted little pumpkins; licked jelly beans stuck on the carpet; apple core in the toy box; rotten bananas; old chicken bones on the window sill; dead frogs; poop skid marks all over the carpet under the bed; collection of nail clippings; cup of dead worms in the window sill; painted contents of a diaper on the wall; leftover chicken under the bed; half-eaten piece of cake so hard it was concrete; sixty dirty smelly socks; a bowl of dried-up dirt; rock-hard, petrified piece of salami under the bed; decaying caterpillar in daughter's room (because she kept hoping it would turn into a butterfly); and a collection of clams from church camp.

Okay! So are you feeling any better about the condition of your child's bedroom? I've never found anything quite so bad, but we have excavated our fair share of keepsakes gone bad, dirty or wet underwear hidden in the back of a closet, and sippy cups with curdled milk! My friend Kelly found that her three-year-old daughter got into her lipstick and used it to "fingerpaint" her hands. She then put a big lipstick handprint on the wall of her bedroom. When Kelly discovered her daughter's "artwork," she thought about painting over it. Instead she decided to draw a pink heart around it and date it. It remained until they repainted the room a few years later!

Different moms have different standards when it comes to bedrooms. Some require beds to be made, the room to have some sense of organization, and clothes put away. Others determine that it's not a hill worth dying on and just close the door. I sit somewhere in between. When there were seven of us under one roof, there was a lot of clutter to be dealt with both inside and outside of the bedrooms!

. . . .

I do believe the foundations of organization get laid in the growing-up years. What we do as moms is not only for our own sanity but also for the benefit of our children's future housekeeping abilities! However, sometimes this can be a tough battle, especially as children get older, have more outside-of-the-home activities, and strong-willed, opinionated personalities to boot!

Since I have the benefit of having both grown children and two teenagers still at home, let me tell you that I often clashed with my three grown children about the condition of their bedrooms. Now they have homes of their own, and they take care of their homes very well. There is hope! When you are frustrated with your children over the condition of their bedrooms, remember that this issue is one-part immaturity, one-part personality, one-part lack of time management, and one-part they-just-don't-care! Keeping this in the back of our minds gives us a balanced perspective.

Kids and clutter just go together. Their "stuff" is important to them. It's part of who they are and who they are becoming. Our goal as moms is to help them learn to manage their personal items in a way that sets good lifetime habits in place. However, we must also make peace with the reality that perfection doesn't exist. In fact, it's unhealthy for your relationship with your children for you to expect it.

Do you make the bed or not? This is a personal preference question. There's not a right or wrong answer. If you decide this is important, you can start teaching them how to do this during the preschool years. In fact, there's a fun way to do this! When they wake up in the morning, teach them to pull the sheet up to their chin. Then pull the blanket, comforter, or bedspread up to their chin. Then, have them try to get out

. . . .

of their bed without messing up the covers they've just pulled up! They usually find this a fun challenge. Once out of bed, show them how to straighten each side of the bed and how to put the pillow on top of the covers. It's done!

Now don't fix the child's imperfectly made bed! Affirm that they did it and leave it the way it is. This gives them a sense of accomplishment. When we impose our desire for perfection upon our children, we discourage them from even trying because they feel they can never measure up. There's nothing worse than children feeling they are never "good enough" for their mom.

What about toys, school papers, and other bedroom items? Do these bits and pieces have a "home"? Does your child know where that "home" is? Open baskets for toys make cleanup easier. A box for special school papers can be helpful (only for special keepsake papers, not *every* school paper — make sure your kids know they can throw away most of their school papers!). A shoebox for special trinkets that don't fit into any other category can also be helpful. Once the shoebox is full, they have to take something out before putting something new in.

How often do you pick up and organize bedrooms? Again, this is personal preference. Some of us are bothered by clutter more than others. When the kids were little, we picked up toys every night. We sang a little cleanup song each night as we worked together to put all the toys away in their bedrooms and other living areas of the house. Now that

Your way is the right way for you and your family.

my boys are teenagers, we clean bedrooms every Saturday. I have them change their bedsheets, dust, organize, put away clothes, and vacuum. Occasionally, we do that every other Saturday. Beyond that, I say little about their bedrooms—no matter what condition they are in. That works for me. What's important is to find what works for you.

Don't compare yourself to me, to your best friend, or to your neighbor. Really evaluate what is important to *you*, and then lead your family accordingly. Be confident that your way is the right way for you and your family.

LAUNDRY

Ah, the joys of laundry! It's always on my to-do list, and I bet it is on yours, too! If only my family would understand the value of going naked for a few days! It would do so much for my sense of accomplishment!

Our family has lived in six different homes over the years. I've done laundry at the Laundromat, at a shared laundry area in an apartment complex, in an unfinished room in our basement, and in a "laundry area" in the upstairs hallway of our current home. I've never had a true laundry room with a specific place to fold laundry so my "laundry folding table" has always been the bed in our master bedroom.

Laundry, it seems, is always spread out in several parts of the house. There are the baskets of laundry that need to be sorted, the loads-waiting-to-go-in-the-washer piles, the washed-but-not-yet-folded piles, and the folded-but-not-yet-put-away piles. Thus the challenge of never feeling like laundry is done!

True confession: writing this section just reminded me of the load of laundry I put in the washer yesterday but forgot to move to the dryer! So I just put the computer down and ran upstairs to move the load from the washer to the dryer! Yep, there are no perfect houses and no perfect moms!

Need some tips to manage laundry better? Try some of these from moms in the trenches:

Set the kitchen timer when you put a load in the washer or the dryer. This will remind you when the load is done and prompt you either to move the load from the washer to the dryer or fold the load that is dried. (I should have used that tip yesterday!)

Use your laundry folding time as a prayer time. Pray for each member of the family as you fold that person's clothes.

Keep a spray bottle of water in the laundry area for spritzing clothes that are wrinkly from being left in the dryer for too long (maybe several days!). Spritz right into the load in the dryer, fluff for five-to-ten minutes, and then fold!

Have your grade-school and older kids help with laundry as much as possible. They wear the clothes so they can help take care of the clothes!

LIVING AREAS

We all live in different-sized homes. In addition to the kitchen, bathrooms, and bedrooms, some of us have a living room, family room, rec room, and dining room. Others of us have one room that serves all of those purposes! Regardless of the size of your home, these living areas are shared by the entire family. They also tend to be the "most seen" rooms of the house.

There are no perfect homes, so you have to determine what level of organization and cleanliness works for your family. Don't let the magazine covers determine that. Don't let your neighbor's level of neatness and organization drive your desire. Don't let my stories determine that level. Seeing the strategies others have implemented and hearing how other moms organize their homes can help you determine what's best for you. However, don't let their standards determine your standards. Use your community for ideas and inspiration, but resist the temptation to measure yourself against others when it comes to your home.

I'm naturally a "messy." I easily make piles and procrastinate cleaning and organizing. However, I began to realize that natural tendency was causing a lot of stress for me. I wanted to find a happy medium, and I have done so by borrowing ideas from my friend and neighbor Crystal. I'll never be as organized as Crystal, but I *can* learn great strategies from her! She's not a better mom than I am because she's better organized and everything in her home has a sense of "design" to it. And I'm not a better mom than she is because I let some things go that she would never stand for. We are two different people who equally love our families. We have different organizational skills, different decorating preferences and knowledge, different ages and stages of kids, and different lifestyles to some extent. Those differences are designed to complement one another, not cause us to compete with one another! We need to learn from other moms, but not compare ourselves to them.

Several years ago, I was introduced to the term *company-ready*. Someone told me she had two rooms in the house (kitchen and living room) that she asked her family to help her keep company-ready. These were the two rooms where she'd likely chat with the neighbor who dropped by unexpectedly, or where she'd talk briefly with the parent of one of her kids' friends who came to pick up the child after a visit. By having these rooms company-ready, (generally picked up and tidied to a comfortable standard), she wasn't stressed when someone unexpectedly came over. She didn't need to apologize for the condition of her house, and she was comfortable with having someone in her home. I really liked that idea and adapted it for our family. What a difference it made in getting my family's buy-in! Now they understood why I wanted things picked up! Not only that, but when I say, "Let's get these rooms company-ready," they know what that means!

Other moms aren't bothered by the "lived in" look. When someone unexpectedly drops by, they invite them in and don't worry about the house or they simply say, "We live in our house; here, let me move a couple of things so you can sit down!" Both of these approaches to the living spaces in our homes are acceptable. Whatever you are comfortable with is right for you, even if it is different from other moms you know!

BUT I WANT HER HOUSE!

When Anne was six, Evan was four, and Erica was a newborn, we lived in a two-bedroom townhouse we rented. Having two kids in a small bedroom was doable, but adding a crib to the already crowded bedroom was craziness. The last thing we wanted was the baby to wake up the other kids, who then couldn't go back to sleep! I truly thought I'd go crazy!

Several of our friends who had also been renting were now buying houses. Mark was just graduating from Bible college, and we were paying his school loans rather than saving for a house. I was so discouraged.

Coveting makes us blind to all that we already have.

I just wanted what everyone else seemed to have: our own yard, space to really live in, a kitchen bigger than a postage stamp, a garage, and a place to call our own!

Why is it we're always wanting something we can't have or maybe don't really need? Why can't we just be content with what we do have? I believe it comes down to the comparison game. When we see someone else's house and ours doesn't seem to measure up, we become discontent. Coveting makes us blind to all that we already have.

Here's something else to consider: We aren't comparing fairly either. We want the house, but do we also want the mortgage payment? What about the upkeep on the bigger yard? How about the property taxes?

I'm thankful that we eventually were able to get into our first house and then several years later were able to move out to the country farmhouse we now live in. But looking back, I now know that little townhouse offered more than I could see at the time:

Fair rent and no property taxes. This alone made a big difference in me being able to be home with my kids during this season of our lives.

Back exit onto a park so my kids had a place to play, but we didn't have to mow the lawn.

No maintenance expenses. If something broke, we called the landlord.

Limited space to clean. Our square footage wasn't too big to take care of with three little ones.

A *great central location* close to our church.

Good neighbors.

Are you in a mobile home, an apartment, a small house, or even your in-laws' basement? What benefits do you have in your current living arrangement? How can you embrace the real living arrangements you have instead of wanting something different?

There's nothing wrong with having a vision you hope to attain or a goal you want to work toward. Just make sure you're doing the right thing for your family and your finances, and that you are doing it for the right reasons.

HOUSE BEAUTIFUL

Being in full-time church ministry for more than twenty years, I've been in hundreds of people's homes. I've also caught myself comparing and being jealous of what they have and I don't have. However, I've seen some very well-to-do families with empty, dysfunctional relationships. I've also seen families struggling financially who have rich, deep, healthy family relationships.

It's not the size, style, décor, or classiness of a house that really matters. It's what goes on inside the house that makes the most difference. A house doesn't make a family. A family makes a house a home.

Do you want a beautiful home? Sure, take care of the physical space you have: Maintain it, clean it on occasion, and keep it organized enough to find what you need to find. More than anything, however, focus on the people living inside those walls. When you get right down to it, it's those flawed yet precious family relationships that make your house truly beautiful.

CHANGE YOUR EXPECTATIONS

We're looking for realistic expectations, not lower expectations. People who live in a space make messes. They leave things out. They get things dirty. Houses get cluttered, dirty, and disorganized. That is real life.

Be careful of expecting perfection from your family when it comes to the condition of your home. Some nights it's okay to throw your clothes on a chair instead of hanging them up. Sometimes the condition of our living space needs to ebb and flow with the demands of life. For instance, when I'm writing a book, I let my desk get far more cluttered than I like it to be on a daily basis. I haven't dusted my bedroom in nearly a month and, yes, I could write my husband a love letter on the surface of our dresser. My expectations change because my reality changes. You can do that, too. When your calendar fills up, or you add a new baby to the family, or you take on work outside the home, or you're dealing with a family member's medical crisis, cut yourself some slack and change your expectations—either expectations about the condition of your home that you'll be okay with or your expectations about how you will accomplish the housekeeping task. You might be able to keep up with things on a regular basis, but if company is coming or the calendar is full, you might need to ask your family to help with some chores they don't normally do.

Change your expectations to meet your reality. You'll do yourself a huge favor. Not only that, but your family will thank you because it will lower the stress in your home.

APPLY THE ANTIDOTE

Dealing with our material things can bring out pride, fear, insecurity, and judgment. Once you've tackled changing your expectations, examine your heart in order to make peace with the condition of your home.

Replace Pride with Humility

Pride has a lot to do with our appearances, including our homes. Work to humble yourself by:

> *Throwing a No-More-Perfect-Moms party!* Tell the moms you invite what you *won't* do (I won't clean my house, manicure my yard, or even fix the peeling wallpaper in my bathroom for this party. However, I'm sure we'll still have a great night of fun!). Then do what you promised and have some women over to your imperfect house.

> *Asking God to show you where pride creeps into your heart as it pertains to your home.* Do you feel "less than" or "better than" someone because of the neighborhood you live in? The size of your house? The condition of your yard? Ask God to help you be grateful for what you have and resist the urge to define yourself positively or negatively based upon where you live.

Replace Fear with Courage

Don't be fearful of having someone in your less-than-perfect home. Remember that dishes on your counter will make her feel better about the dishes she left on her counter! Increase your courage by:

Setting a date on the calendar to have a friend over. If you're not comfortable entertaining in your home, invite her over to sit in the sun and let the kids run in the sprinkler. I invite friends over to sit on the porch and enjoy a glass of iced tea in the summer. It's the shared company we look forward to the most!

How clean your kitchen floor is does not define you.

Choosing not *to do something you would normally do when getting ready for company.* What is the worst that could happen if you didn't mop the kitchen floor before your mother-in-law visited? Even if she were to make a remark about it, could you respond in a way that communicates your efforts to be realistic about your expectations and your desire to put people before tasks?

Replace Insecurity with Confidence

The size or condition of your house does not define you. The neighborhood you live in does not define you. How clean your kitchen floor is does not define you. Don't let the lack of or the condition of material things cause you insecurity. Increase your confidence by:

Creating a gratefulness journal or a God Box. Write down in a journal the blessings in your life. When you want to complain, ask God, "What is good about my situation?" (For example, see that list of the blessings of living in that small townhouse.) A *God Box* is a shadow box or treasure chest you display prominently in your home. Inside the box you put a trinket or visual reminder of something you are grateful for. When we increase our gratitude, we keep our hearts soft and pliable for God to do His best work. First Timothy 4:4 reminds us of the importance of thanksgiving: "For everything God created is good, and nothing is to be rejected if it is received with thanksgiving."

Reminding yourself of your value in God's eyes. The condition of your house will change every day. If little ones are in your home, the condition of your house will likely change nearly every minute! Don't let changing conditions define you; let an unchanging God define you. God says He will never leave you nor forsake you (Deuteronomy 31:6). Even when your dishes aren't done, and your shoes stick to your kitchen floor, God's love for you will never change!

Replace Judgment with Grace

Most of the time when we need to replace judgment with grace it has something to do with the way we see and judge other people. However, this time, the person you need to stop judging is yourself. Most moms are very hard on themselves when it comes to their homes. If you are one of those moms who feels others have it more together when it comes to that place called home, you can increase the grace you give yourself by:

Paying attention to the messages in your head. What are you telling yourself about your house? What critical statements are you repeating over and over that only you can hear? Our inner thoughts control how we feel about ourselves, and too often they can be so destructive. When a judgmental thought pops into your mind, replace it with a grace-giving thought. For instance, if you think, *I'm such a mom-failure. Why can't I keep my kitchen cleaned up?* replace it with something like, *The kitchen is hard to stay on top of because it's the center of our home. Today, I'm giving myself grace because I have chosen to live out the principle that people are more important than projects.*

Watching the video called "Jill's House Tour" at NoMorePer fectMoms.com. Find reassurance in another mom's imperfect, well-lived-in house!

EMBRACE YOUR BEAUTIFUL, IMPERFECT HOME

Have you ever considered the home you have compared to what moms have in emerging countries? Have you thought about what it would be like to live in a mud hut and sleep on a mat on the floor? Have you thanked God today for clean running water and the indoor plumbing you and your family enjoy? If you sleep in a bed and have a blanket to cover yourself, you have more than many moms in this world.

There are no perfect homes — just imperfect, sometimes-messy places where our families can gather and love on one another.

CHAPTER 9

NO MORE *Perfect* HOMEMAKING

van's high school had an "open lunch," which allowed students to leave the campus to go home or out to a restaurant for lunch. This particular day he was bringing a friend home for lunch and asked me if I'd have grilled cheese sandwiches waiting for them. As usual, I had twenty things going at the same time: laundry, emails, phone conversations, and more. I had noted the time and knew I needed to get the sandwiches cooking. I buttered the bread, slapped the cheese between the two slices, and put them on the hot griddle. Then the phone rang. I stood by the stove and talked to the caller, but then mindlessly walked away as I continued the conversation. I never saw Evan's car pull in the driveway. He pulled in the garage and as soon as he exited the car, he could smell the burnt sandwiches. "Oh no," he announced to his

....

friend. "My mom has burnt the grilled cheese *again*."

Yep. Perfection went right out the window.

MEALS

We've all done it. We had perfect plans for a meal and the recipe flopped, or we didn't allow enough time, or we lacked in cooking skills, or we were distracted by a crying child, or we were trying to do too many things at once.

Food is necessary for living. We need to eat on a regular basis, so making meals is always on a mom's "to do" list. There's breakfast, then sometimes a mid-morning snack, then lunch, then an afternoon snack, then dinner, and then some of us put together a before-bedtime snack. Providing all of those snacks and meals seems to be a full-time job in and of itself!

However, eating isn't all about the food. It's also about connection. Many conversations happen around the dinner table. Laughter happens when funny stories are shared. Encouragement is given when challenges are faced. Sitting at the dinner table, we occasionally find out what's going on in the hearts and minds of the family members who mean so much to us. Even when my son brought his friend home for lunch, it wasn't really about the food for me; it was about the slice of time I got to share with him in the middle of a school day. (Yes, I did throw out the burnt sandwiches and made the boys edible ones instead!)

With cable television and the Web, cooking demonstrations are more available to the average person than in the past. That's good news for those of us who need some basic meal-prep skills. However, it also resurrects that age-old challenge: the temptation to compare.

I don't often watch the Food Network, but I do occasionally catch a show. I'll admit, when I watch my favorites, the comparisons start right away. *How in the world does she make all these wonderful dishes and remain the size of a toothpick?* Yep, you got it. It's a show about learning to make yummy food, and I'm making it about body image! Aaargh! We are always battling the Perfection Infection!

Even if we watch to learn, we still sometimes unconsciously compare our real lives to the show. We think thoughts like: *If I had that kitchen, I could make that meal, too.* Or, *Oh I wish I had a food processor!* Or, *Why didn't my mom teach me to cook?* Or, *Why do they make it look so easy when it always feels so hard to me?* We're comparing our real challenges to their "picture perfect" meals made in thirty minutes!

Let's paint a real picture of what happens on these cooking shows: Someone else cuts up the vegetables. Someone measures out all the ingredients into little prep bowls. Someone prepares the whole dish ahead of time so the chef can show you how to assemble the recipe, put it in the oven or start to cook it on the stove, and then presto, they produce a perfect finished product! Wow! If it was really only as easy as they show it on TV!

I've never seen a cooking show with a mom carrying a baby in a sling to keep him from crying while she's making gravy. I've never seen a cooking show where the chef has a toddler clinging to her leg while she makes a scrumptious stew. I've never seen a cooking show where the chef serves up the food to her moody teenagers who can't seem to find anything nice to say about anything at all. While these shows are great for ideas and even education, we have to be careful that they don't

. . . .

create a feeling that we don't measure up. We have to be aware of our tendency to compare and come out wanting once again.

So what's a busy mom to do? I enjoy baking, but I honestly don't like cooking. It feels like a lot of work that just goes down the tube — literally. Of course, my family needs to eat and so do I, so providing meals is something that needs to happen.

However, I have to be true to who I am, and you do, too. We have to give ourselves grace, work within our skill and desire level, and have realistic expectations of what we can and cannot do. I have met women who line up all along the spectrum of meal-making strategies. On one end of the spectrum is a working mom I know who makes no meals at home at all. She doesn't apologize for this. In fact, it's a boundary she has decided is important for her to keep a balance in her life as a working mom. She can't be all things to all people. This works for her because they share a house with extended family and her mom does the majority of the meal-making. The whole family usually eats together in the evening. What meals her mom doesn't cook, they eat out.

Let's not judge one another, and let's not judge ourselves.

Another mom I know was taking her family out to eat every meal, but not for the same reason. This mom didn't know how to cook at all. Her own mother didn't cook, and she never learned how. But she wasn't content, so she decided to do something about it. She asked for help, sought instruction online, and determined to change things in her home.

A stay-at-home mom I know cooks nearly every meal at home. Eating out is reserved for special occasions like birthdays. Their limited budget doesn't allow for eating out, so she stays within budget and feels that cooking at home is actually one way she "earns" money for her family.

As you can see, there are moms all along the spectrum of "normal" meal-making. Let's not judge one another, and let's not judge ourselves. Let's figure out what's best for us and for our families, set our strategies in place, and enjoy our imperfect but beautiful meals together as often as possible.

There are no perfect meals, but there are ways to streamline the meal-making process. To minimize the stress of meal prep, try some of these strategies from moms in the trenches:

Prep in bulk. Brown ground hamburger or ground turkey when you bring it home from the store. Then freeze it in "recipe" sized containers. This makes assembling a casserole or making chili a breeze. Does your family enjoy Mexican? Go ahead and season the browned meat and freeze it. Do you like to add sausage to scrambled eggs, homemade pizza, quiche, or biscuits and sausage gravy? Brown some sausage in bulk and freeze it browned so it's ready to toss into one of your favorite sausage recipes!

Use the Crock-Pot. The Crock-Pot only requires that you think ahead (which is hard for many of us!). The best part is that you can "fix and forget." Now that's my kind of meal making! Need ideas? Check out the "Crockin' Girls" on Facebook!

Think outside the box. Breakfast for dinner? It's a family favorite at the Savage household! Cereal for lunch? If it's nutritious enough for breakfast, it works for lunch, too!

Use fresh veggies. Rather than cooking a vegetable, serve a salad. A salad is a healthy choice that's quick to prepare. Keep fun salad toppings on hand like dried cranberries, sunflower kernels, and sliced almonds to fancy up a salad. You can throw fruit on a salad, too! Chopped apples, mandarin oranges, and strawberries are not only nutritious, but yummy additions to a salad.

Create a monthly meal plan. Determine thirty days of meals that your family enjoys. Then use the monthly meal plan template each month. No need to rethink what you've already thought out well!

Let someone else in the family share the cooking responsibilities. If your husband enjoys cooking, let him share the love! If you have a teenager, let him or her cook regularly to strengthen this life skill.

DECORATING

Years ago, a friend and I spent a day wadding up Saran Wrap, dipping it in paint, and painting a faux finish on the walls in my stairway and hallway. The finish is beautiful, and it cost me just $15 for the plastic wrap and the paint. Painting is not my favorite project to tackle, but the finished job was worth the effort. Not only that, the marbled look on my walls hides dirty fingerprints perfectly!

I'm not much of a creative thinker when it comes to decorating. But I can "borrow" a great idea any day! Of course, I can play that comparison game and find myself feeling like a failure in the "home decorating" area of my life. However, I can also realize that God's given the gift of decorating creativity to others so they can share it with me!

There are days when the comparison game sneaks in, and I hardly realize I'm on the condemnation road until I'm battling the lies. Like the other day when my friend Crystal told me about a bulletin board she had made. She'd printed out some pictures and hung them on the decorative bulletin board in her daughter's bedroom. In my head and before I realized it was happening, I thought to myself, *Of course you did that. I've had some pictures I've wanted to hang in our toy room for over a year. Do I have that project done? Nope, I don't. Why can you get those projects done? You have four younger kids at home, and I just have two teens at home. I should be able to get something like that accomplished, too. I'm such a loser!*

Oh, the negative self-talk that creeps into our hearts and minds! For some of us, it's been there for so long, we hardly see it as a problem. It's an old friend. Because of its familiarity, we invite the voice in and offer it a meal rather than recognizing it as destructive and kicking it out on the street where it belongs.

If I could have used Crystal's accomplishment to motivate me to do my project, that would have been helpful. Sharing her idea would have prompted conviction—or accountability—in me. It would have been a welcome reminder to prioritize that project. Instead, I used her

· · · · · · · ·

accomplishment to compare my insides to her outsides. It was an unfair comparison that instead brought condemnation to my heart.

That hasn't always happened. I remember when my friend Shawn invited me over to see how she had decorated her preschool son's room. I was amazed at the simple creativity she had used! Shawn wanted to decorate Nathan's room with a jungle theme. She visualized all kinds of animals painted on the walls: a lion, tiger, elephant, and monkey. Shawn found some pictures of the animals she had in mind. After turning the pictures into overhead transparencies (a service offered at any teacher supply store or print shop), she used an overhead projector to project the figures on the bedroom walls. The next step involved tracing the projected figures with a pencil. After that, the figures were painted and details added using the pictures as a template. When the room was finished, the animal figures reached from floor to ceiling in the one-of-a-kind bedroom. Shawn's project inspired me to think creatively!

My friend and former neighbor Rita also has a creative flair with decorating. She makes a hobby out of finding old and often discarded furniture and bringing new life to it. I've seen her take iron bed frames, old chairs, and discarded tables and make them into useful pieces of furniture. With the wide variety of paint products and special paint effects available, this type of creative project can be accomplished by almost anyone. Seeing Rita's projects has caused me to look for possibilities in something that seems to be at the end of its useful life. Because of Rita, I now use an old trunk that I inherited from my grandmother as a storage space for the blankets in our family room.

When it comes to decorating, we have to guard against the

temptation to compare. Our homes are unique to our families. We don't want a carbon copy of someone else's home. We want what works for us and for our particular family. Whether decorating comes easily for you, or it's a challenge, balance inspirations with resisting the urge to compare—and do only what's right for you and your family.

HOSPITALITY

Hospitality is a term usually associated with how we treat guests in our homes. I like to think of it as how we treat friends and family both inside and outside our home. Hospitality is our opportunity to be Jesus to those around us.

We have to be careful with the concept of hospitality because unrealistic expectations can come into play here. Whether it's hosting the extended family Thanksgiving dinner or just making our kids' friends feel at home in our houses, our expectations can be set so high that we can only see our failures.

The "burned grilled cheese" story seems like a failed attempt at hospitality. I could look at it that way. However, I actually don't. After I threw away the burnt sandwiches and made new ones, I sat at the table with Evan and his friend and had a great conversation with them both. It was definitely not a perfect extension of hospitality, but it was hospitality nonetheless. I also didn't ruin the opportunity for future hospitality; there were plenty of other times Evan called about eating lunch at home and I managed to get the food right on the first try!

Too often we talk ourselves right out of hospitality because we fear that our efforts won't measure up. Measure up to what? That elusive "perfect picture" we have in our minds of what our houses need to look like, what kind of food we need to serve, or even how we want our kids to behave. One mom put it this way, "I don't have people over because I don't keep my house looking like a page out of *Better Homes and Gardens*. I am a clutter hound, and we have so much stuff. Everything seems to be in place at other moms' houses, but never at mine!"

When I asked my Facebook friends what kept them from inviting someone over, the honest responses were overwhelming: "My house isn't good enough." "I'm not a 'fancy' cook." "My home and belongings don't measure up." "I'm afraid the food I serve will not be good enough." "I'm afraid people won't have fun." "I'm afraid they will say no and I will be rejected." One mom drew this equation: "It has to be perfect to have someone over + it's never perfect = never having people over." Wow, so many of us are afraid of something when it comes to extending hospitality! We allow our fears to control us and our expectations to paralyze us, which keeps us isolated and disconnected from the relationships we need the most.

I loved hearing some honest responses from the other angle. One mom gave this encouragement, "I have about three meals I'm good at for a crowd, and I stick to those. Get good at a couple of things, and change up the sides." Heather said, "We have company all the time! Coffee dates, popcorn night, pancakes (I had sixteen people over! We made pancakes and had a blast!), game nights . . . open up your heart and your home, and you'll find most people could really care less what your house looks like!" Even my daughter Erica said, "When my husband first offered our home as a meeting place for our small group every week, I freaked out at having people in our home every week. I thought they'd think our garage-sale furniture was old or not comfortable. But I pushed through the fear and now two months down the road, I've realized that no one has complained that the house isn't perfect or the couch isn't comfortable. Our group is growing, and so are our friendships!"

Simplify.
Simplify.
Simplify.

I've learned to keep a box of frozen burgers and a package of hamburger buns in my freezer at all times. That's my standard "company" meal. We grill the burgers (we put them right on the grill frozen!), I open up a bag of chips, warm up some baked beans (if I have them) or put out some baby carrots. It's nothing fancy, but it gets us around the table or chatting while we eat on the porch in the summer. If I'm really energetic, I'll throw some boxed brownies in the oven for dessert. However, I've had company over and not served dessert, too! Simplify. Simplify. Simplify.

At the same time, there are plenty of times when I'd like to invite someone over but I just don't have the energy. Or I don't want to make the effort. Or I've become so comfortable in my now "almost empty nest" that I don't want to change up my comfy, predictable routine.

I'm going to take a risk and maybe even step on our toes for a bit. Is our resistance to hospitality and allowing our fears to control us really an act of selfishness? Are we caring more about how we feel than how our hospitality may make the other person feel? One mom shared, "I was just invited over for the first time by someone I barely know, and I felt so thankful and honored. Just her invite is enough to make me feel a little special."

Could we open ourselves up to the possibility of extending hospitality by thinking about how the invited person would feel rather than how we will feel? Can we stretch ourselves enough to face our fears and expand our network of friends? What if we started with a baby step of simply inviting someone over to let the kids play in the yard and sharing some lemonade? Or maybe just inviting another mom to meet you for a picnic at a park? That's hospitality, too! It doesn't always have to involve the house; hospitality is an extension of our hearts!

In her book *A Life That Says Welcome*, Karen Ehman reminds us that "entertaining puts the emphasis on you and how you can impress others. Offering hospitality puts the emphasis on others and strives to meet their physical and spiritual needs so that they feel refreshed, not impressed, when they leave your home."[1] I love how Karen puts it! She takes the focus off of us and puts it on the guest. That's what hospitality is all about!

CHANGE YOUR EXPECTATIONS

When it comes to homemaking, it's time we cut ourselves some slack. Real meals are sometimes thrown together. Real homes are decorated with pictures drawn by a two-year-old holding a red crayon. Real hospitality can be a simple effort to live a life that says, "Welcome!"

It's not about lowering our expectations. It's about changing our expectations to something more realistic. I'm hosting a Thursday night Bible study at my house right now. The group meets at 7:00, and many times at 6:30 my kitchen looks like a disaster area. Sometimes the group arrives and there are dishes sitting in the sink, clean dishes in the drainer that need to be put away, and piles of paper on my counters. My goal is to "organize the clutter" enough that there's a place for someone to sit at my kitchen island, fix a cup of tea, and chat for a few minutes until we move to the living room or porch. Once the clutter is organized, I wipe the counters so nobody puts their hand in something sticky—and then I call it done! I used to expect perfection, and I about killed my family and myself pursuing that elusive goal. Now I expect "organized reality," and I find having people over is far less stressful!

APPLY THE ANTIDOTE

Making meals, decorating, and extending hospitality are all a part of making a home. They are also all areas where the Perfection Infection runs rampant and keeps us from being all God wants us to be. However, there is hope and progress to be made. If we apply the antidotes to our everyday challenges, we can rid ourselves of this ugly disease and find the freedom in authenticity we long for.

Progress from Fear to Courage

Fear keeps us from doing something differently. It paralyzes us. It keeps us from growing, learning, and reaching out to others. If fear is paralyzing you in the kitchen, start doing something about it. Watch the Food Network. Pick up a cooking magazine. Ask your Facebook friends for their favorite easy main dish recipe.

If fear is keeping you from doing something to kick up the décor in your home, ask for help. I have several friends who decorate their homes beautifully. When I want to do something fresh in a room, I'll muster up the courage to ask one of them over saying, "Help me! What can I do differently in this room with what I already have?" A fresh eye can see all kinds of ideas! If you can't even think about décor and it's the clutter that's bothering you, you've got to start somewhere! My kids used to tell this joke, "How do you eat an elephant?" The answer is,

"One bite at a time." The same thing can be said about cleaning up clutter. Take it one room, one corner, even one stack of papers at a time! Be courageous, and move fear aside!

If reaching out to others is where fear stops you, take a first step by asking a mom to meet you somewhere away from your home. Push through your fear of rejection and extend a hand of friendship. If she says no, ask someone else. Resist the urge to take that no answer personally; her schedule just might not allow the time for whatever activity you suggested. If you'd really like to find courage and feel equipped to open up your heart and home, get a copy of Karen Ehman's book *A Life That Says Welcome*. It will change your perspective and build your courage to open up your heart and home to others.

Progress from Insecurity to Confidence

Women tend to feel most insecure about body image and home image. We all struggle with insecurity about our homemaking in some way. Other women are better cooks than we are. Other moms have a better eye for decorating than we do. Other women seem more interesting than we are. The lies we've been telling ourselves for years are so familiar.

Notice the word I used to describe moving from insecurity to confidence: *progress*. We don't move from insecurity to confidence in any area of our lives overnight. It's a progression of taking a risk, feeling success (now that wasn't so bad!), taking another risk, feeling another success, taking another risk, experiencing a setback when things didn't go as we hoped (this is reality, right?), and taking yet another risk. These baby steps of courage help

We are our own worst critics!

us progress from insecurity to confidence. In the words of hospitality author and speaker Tammy Maltby, "Start simply, and simply start."

Progress from Judgment to Grace

Let's face it: We are our own worst critics! However, most of us don't think of that as judging ourselves. We usually think of judging as something we do to other people. However, if we are going to tackle the Perfection Infection in our homemaking, we need to progress from judgment to grace in our own self-criticism.

What you say and think to yourself becomes what you feel. What you feel becomes what you believe. However, our thoughts and feelings don't always tell us the truth. Take these steps to make progress in giving yourself grace:

Start with self-awareness. Being aware of the negative voice in your head is the first step to silencing your inner critic. What is that negative voice declaring?

Change each declaration into a question that motivates. If your inner critic says, "I'll never be a good cook!" change that into the question, "How can I become a good cook?" If your judging voice says, "You're no good at conversation. It will be a failure to invite someone over," change that to, "What can I do to be better at conversation? What questions can I ask so I can have a successful conversation?"

Accept God's grace as a gift. You don't have to earn it! Accept His grace—His love for you in spite of your human shortcomings—and then give that grace to yourself. Accept your flaws. Embrace your growth opportunities. Enjoy the freedom found in authentic living.

Take a baby step. One baby step plus another baby step will slowly move you from insecurity to confidence in the art of homemaking.

EMBRACE YOUR BEAUTIFUL, IMPERFECT HOMEMAKING SKILLS

June Cleaver doesn't exist. She never did. The *Leave It to Beaver* actress also had to go home to dirty dishes in the sink and toilets that needed to be scrubbed. She had to figure out what was for dinner and decorated her house on a budget, too.

There are no perfect homemakers—just real moms, deciding what's right for their families and working to create a warm, nurturing home for those they love.

Note

1. Karen Ehman, *A Life That Says Welcome* (Grand Rapids: Revell, 2006), 18.

CHAPTER 10

ONE *Perfect* GOD

What a journey we've been on! I hope you've come to understand, as I have, that unrealistic expectations about our real, imperfect life, set us up for a great deal of disappointment if we're not aware of them. We've also seen the damage that comparison does in our hearts and our minds. We've discovered that we're not alone in the real stuff of life and that it's okay to be honest about our challenges. We've explored the reality of the Perfection Infection and how pervasive it is in our culture and in our own relationships. We've also learned about the antidotes that can help us eradicate this terrible condition.

Our imperfect lives are counterbalanced with a perfect God.

While we've spent a lot of time disassembling perfection and rooting out unrealistic expectations, there is another part of this expedition we must explore before considering the topic fully covered. We must understand that the imperfect parts of our lives are counterbalanced with the reality of a perfect God who longs to shine His light through the cracks in our lives.

With God, we can go ahead and have high expectations. As we let go of the unrealistic expectations that keep getting us in trouble, we can turn to expectancy that will never fail us. Expectancy indicates anticipation—looking forward to something. We can safely anticipate that God is at work and doing something!

We can't be perfect parents, but we can act in partnership with a perfect God. There is peace, hope, and expectancy in that statement. Let's take a look at what this perfect God gives to moms like you and me—sometimes weary, often overwhelmed, and always imperfect.

GOD'S PERFECT LOVE

Love. It's a word easily thrown around in our everyday language. We say things like, "I love that movie!" or "I love chocolate ice cream!" or "I'd love to know you better." However, the use of *love* in those statements doesn't even come close to the way God loves us. His love is perfect because it is unchanging and unconditional. Even in our best moments, we have a long way to go to learn to love like God loves.

God's love is unchanging. There is nothing we can do to make God love us more, and there is nothing we can do to make God love us less. That's really hard for most of us to understand because we haven't been loved in a similar way in our human relationships. Human feelings complicate human expressions of love. Have you ever said, "I love him, but I don't like him right now." I know I've said that about my husband or each one of my children at one time or another.

Guess what? God never says that about you or me. He would never say that no matter what we did because His love is perfect. His feelings about us don't differ when we've had a good mothering day or when we've blown it with our kids. His love simply does not change.

Yet there's more good news! God's love is also unconditional. God doesn't put conditions on us that require us to "earn" His love. He doesn't say, "Now, Jill, if you don't yell at your kids today, I'll give you My love. But if you do yell at your kids, you're on your own and I won't be showing you My love today." God loves you and me whether we're having a good mothering day or a bad one. That's not an excuse for us to do wrong. In an effort to protect our hearts and the hearts of our husband and children, God certainly wants us to make right choices. But if we blow it, we can trust that God will continue to surround us with love, offer forgiveness, and provide a second chance. He won't withdraw His love from us.

Unconditional love stays steady despite the circumstances. It believes the best and sees the loved one for who that person can be, rather than who that person is right now. Much of the time, love is also undeserved. That's what makes God's love for us a perfect love.

GOD'S PERFECT STRENGTH

Culturally, weakness is considered a fault. It's often seen as a failure. Too often we believe if we are weak in some area of our lives, we're at a disadvantage.

However, God's economy is different. Contrary to the world's viewpoint, God sees weakness as a positive opportunity. He celebrates! Throws a party! He gives us a pat on the back when we admit our weaknesses! Why? Because it's only when we admit our weaknesses that we realize our need for God's strength!

When we're trying to root out the Perfection Infection from our lives, we desperately need God's strength. On our own, we don't have what it takes to successfully move from pride to humility, fear to courage, insecurity to confidence, and judgment to grace. God tells us, "My grace is sufficient for you, for my power is made perfect in weakness" (2 Corinthians 12:9).

I love that truth! His power is made perfect in our weakness. Now that's perfection you and I can actually desire. That perfection isn't unhealthy for us or for our relationships. When God lives in our hearts, He longs to sit in the driver's seat of our lives. His Spirit longs to reside inside of us to perfect us to be more like Him. When I allow God's strength to overcome my weakness, there's a little more of God in me and a little less of me. That's a good thing. John 3:30 confirms this: "He must become greater; I must become less."

Philippians 4:13 offers a truth we can use to apply this concept to everyday life: "I can do everything through Christ, who gives me strength" (NLT). So let's look at a situation that happened over twenty years ago in my life. When I was new in town and knew no one, I applied this truth to help me apply the antidote of courage.

I was feeling terribly lonely. I was a mom of a two-year-old and a four-year-old in a brand new city. I desperately needed to find some friends. Because I'm an introvert, initiating friendships is a scary thing for me to do, but I was trying to move from fear to courage. I talked to God about it: *God, I'm really needing some new friends. You know that's scary territory for me, but You also know I want to be stretched. I want to do something about my loneliness. Your Word tells me I can do all things through You, who gives me strength I don't have. Give me Your strength and bolster my courage as I make this phone call to invite this mom to meet me for coffee.*

When, in our weakness, we ask for God's strength, we really see that God goes to work. God will never force Himself on us. He'll patiently wait until we ask for His help. So I decided to pick up the phone, even though I was scared to death to make the call. When she answered, I told her who I was (we'd met in the church nursery the week before) and gave the invite. She said no, she couldn't. They had a lot on their schedule, and she wasn't adding anything else to her calendar right now.

Rejection! God gave me courage to reach out, and I got rejected on the first try! However, I was determined not to be discouraged. I had met another mom that same day. We'd exchanged phone numbers, so I decide to give her a call. That call went differently. She was thrilled at the opportunity to get out of the house one evening. We met for coffee, and a friendship was born. We didn't become the best of friends, but she began to introduce me to other moms at church. Slowly, but surely, I forged new friendships in our church and community.

Do you need strength? Looking to move from fear to courage or insecurity to confidence? Ask God for His perfect strength. His power is made perfect in our weakness!

GOD'S PERFECT IDENTITY

Thanks to Facebook, this is the first book I've written where I have had a built-in focus group of moms to send me instant feedback when I bounce off questions and ideas. I've determined that Facebook is the biggest moms group in the world! When I was writing the hospitality chapter, I asked this question, "Do you ever talk yourself right out of extending hospitality in some way (having another mom over, inviting another family over for a cookout, etc.)? If so, what are your fears or struggles in doing so?"

Wow! Within minutes I had over fifty responses! Most moms shared honestly that they rarely—if ever—had someone over. The biggest reason was the fear of being judged by someone who would be harshly critical of her home or by someone who wouldn't find them good company.

One friend looking over all the responses commented, "Wow. Isn't it interesting how many of us deal with the fear of man?" I'd never thought of it in those words, but she is right. We are afraid of what others will think of us! If we're honest, it's because we allow other people to define us.

Too often we care about other people's opinions more than God's opinion. We get trapped by this kind of thinking. Can you see how you've been caught in any of these traps?

Fake outward behavior: Because we want to impress people, we try to become someone we really aren't.

Idolatry: When we care more about what people think, we actually start to worship them (we think about them more than we think about God). Our drive for approval turns people into idols.

Timidity: When we worry about what people think, we're less likely to take risks and stretch ourselves for fear of embarrassment.

Dishonesty: If we fear someone's response to our honest communication, we'll ultimately choose to be dishonest because of the words we're unwilling to share.

Loneliness: If we're always afraid of what people will think, we'll choose not to reach out in friendship. We'll find ourselves isolated and living life without the beauty of community.

It's important that we respect others, but not fear them. It's important to honor others, but not worship them. Only God is to be feared and worshiped. We confuse the role God plays in our lives when we depend on people to approve, define, or accept us. Only God gives us an unchangeable, perfect identity.

We can embrace our perfect identity when we're able to see ourselves through God's eyes. This is why reading the Bible is so important. The Bible is God's voice, and we desperately need His voice to drown out the voices of this world.

God doesn't force us into a relationship with Him. He extends His hand and longs for us to take it. Once you grab hold of God's hand, your new identity is in place: You are forgiven. You are protected. You are an overcomer. You are set free. You are growing. You are secure. You can have peace, and so much more! Flip over to appendix A to discover more about your full identity. This is who you are in God's eyes!

The best part about this identity is that it never changes. If you're having a bad day, God doesn't see you any differently. If you make a mistake, God's viewpoint doesn't change. If you feel bad about yourself, you can know without a doubt that God doesn't feel the same way. If someone says something bad about you, God doesn't buy it.

. . . .

Are you weary of being defined by changing circumstances? Are you drained from constantly being afraid of what others think? God's identity will provide you a much-needed respite from the fear of what other people think—as well as the perfect peace you're longing for.

GOD'S PERFECT HOPE

Hope. In a world filled with human relationships and circumstances beyond our control that often feel so hopeless, we long for hope.

We use the word *hope* in our everyday language: I hope it rains tonight. I hope she behaves for the babysitter. I hope he gets the job. That's not the kind of hope God offers us, though. His hope is so much more.

The Bible was originally written in Greek and Hebrew. The languages of Greek and Hebrew have more descriptive words than the English language. In fact, there are several Greek and Hebrew words that translate into the one word we know as *hope*. In the Old Testament the word *hope* has a Hebrew root that means "trust." This is the foundation of Psalm 33:22: "Let your unfailing love surround us, Lord, for our hope is in you alone" (NLT). We can even substitute the word *trust* for the word *hope* in that verse, and we can see how it further paints a picture of how God's love gives us security.

In another place in the Old Testament, the Hebrew word *towcheleth* means "expectation." We see this used in Psalm 39:7: "But now, Lord, what do I look for? My hope is in you." So *hope* means trust and expectation, but that's not all.

In the New Testament, we see yet another root word for *hope*. It's the Greek word *elpis*, meaning "to expect or anticipate with pleasure." We see this kind of hope in Titus 2:13: "We look forward with hope to that wonderful day when the glory of our great God and Savior, Jesus Christ, will be revealed" (NLT). This kind of hope is a guarantee—a sure thing.

So God's hope is trust, expectation, and a guarantee. In a changing world filled with insecurity, this is assurance you and I desperately need. What does this look like in everyday life?

- When you face a broken marriage, God's hope says healing is possible.
- When you face injustice, God's hope says justice will happen.
- When you face grief, God's hope says you will experience joy again.
- When you face betrayal, God's hope says truth will triumph.
- When you face anxiety, God's hope says peace can be found.
- When you face weakness, God's hope says His strength will prevail.
- When you face death, God's hope says there is life after death.

Are you ready to put your trust in a sure thing? Do you long to put worry to rest? Want a guarantee that there's more to this world than meets the eye? God's perfect hope is a promise we most assuredly need.

GOD'S PERFECT TRUTH

What if you wanted to build your family a house right on the beach? Not along the beach, but right on the sand itself. You couldn't do it, right? The reason is that sand does not provide a strong and immovable foundation that will support a building. When the tide comes in, the sand moves. Some of it is carried out to sea, and some of it shifts around.

This is why hotels, houses, and restaurants are built back from the shore, where the footings and foundation can be anchored in solid ground.

This picture is one that God paints for us in Matthew 7:24–27:

> Everyone who hears these words of mine and puts them into practice is like a wise man who built his house on the rock. The rain came down, the streams rose, and the winds blew and beat against that house; yet it did not fall, because it had its foundation on the rock. But everyone who hears these words of mine and does not put them into practice is like a foolish man who built his house on sand. The rain came down, the streams rose, and the winds blew and beat against that house, and it fell with a great crash.

When the floods of life threaten to drown us, God's truth is the life vest that keeps our heads above water.

The "words of mine" the passage refers to is the truth found in the Bible. This is perfect truth that provides a firm foundation for our hearts and our lives. When the winds of life threaten to blow us over, God's truth keeps us secure and unmovable. When the floods of life threaten to drown us in hopelessness, God's truth is the life vest that keeps our heads above water.

God's truth helps us see black and white, right and wrong. Contrary to the prevailing worldview that says truth is grey and relative to how we think or feel, God's truth is absolute. It doesn't change based upon our emotions or opinions. That's what makes it so immovable. Secure. Strong.

The Bible is our instruction book for life. God longs for us to read the directions and follow them. He doesn't promise we'll have a perfect

life, but He does promise us He'll show us how to handle the imperfections of life with grace, hope, love, and integrity. That's why it's
important for us to read the Bible every day.

I once heard someone say that when you read the Bible, you increase the Holy Spirit's vocabulary in your life. I have seen the truth of
this! When Austin was just several weeks old, he had a medical condition that required an MRI. They asked us to deprive him of sleep so he
would sleep during the MRI. (I think our effort to deprive his sleep left
us more sleep-deprived than he was!)

When we arrived at the MRI office, Austin would not sleep for the
test. Finally, the MRI tech said the only way we were going to get this
test accomplished was for me to lie on my back and for Austin to lie on
my tummy. Holding him would cause him to sleep, but it also required
this claustrophobic mother to go in the tube with a baby on her belly.
This was not my idea of fun!

I climbed onto the bed, and the nurse laid Austin on my belly. His
anxiety decreased, and mine began to increase! During this thirty-
minute test we'd be in a narrow tube and unable to move. Immediately
Philippians 4:13 came to my mind: "I can do everything through Christ,
who gives me strength." God was talking to me through His Word! I
said the verse over and over in my head throughout the test. Thirty minutes later, Austin was sound asleep, and I was close to it. God carried
me through this challenge with the truth of His Word.

When my husband left our family for a time, I cried myself to sleep
with my Bible lying next to me. It was the last thing I would read before
I'd go to sleep, and it was the first thing I'd see and read in the morning.
Eventually I intentionally laid it on Mark's pillow every night. It stayed

. . . .

there until he returned home three months later. One of the verses that brought me comfort was Psalm 34:18: "The Lord is close to the brokenhearted and saves those who are crushed in spirit." A verse that brought me hope was Matthew 19:26: "Jesus looked at them and said, 'With man this is impossible, but with God all things are possible.'"

If you're not familiar with the Bible, pick up a version that is easy to read, like the NIV (New International Version) or the NLT (New Living Translation), or even the paraphrased Bible called *The Message*. A great place to start is the book of Proverbs. It's a book filled with practical wisdom that will guide you, encourage you, and stick with you! (Tip: There are thirty-one chapters in Proverbs. If you can read one chapter a day that corresponds with whatever day of the month it is, you'll read the whole book in a month—and then, if you like, you can start over again the next month!) In the book of Matthew, you'll find a biography of Jesus. After you read Matthew, try the book of Philippians. It's short, but power-packed. So is the book of James. You can also find the Bible online at www.biblegateway.com. If you have a smartphone, you can access the free YouVersion Bible app, where you can also tap into all kinds of Bible reading plans. Oh, and if you're looking for a great devotional that keeps you focused on God and His Word, check out Sarah Young's *Jesus Calling* (Thomas Nelson). Available in book form and as a smartphone app, *Jesus Calling* brings God's Word alive as if God is talking directly to you. If you're facing a particular challenge, check out appendix B, "Where to Find Help When You're Feeling—." This great resource can help you find the truth you need when you need it.

Are you trying to build your life on sinking sand? Are the winds of life blowing you over? It's time to sink your roots into God's perfect truth, where you'll find the firm foundation you've been looking for.

GOD'S PERFECT REDEMPTION

Anyone who has used a coupon is familiar with the word *redeem*. When we redeem a coupon we exchange it for something we want. We also redeem airline miles when we exchange the points we've collected for an airline ticket to a place we want to go. Anytime the word *redeem* is used, it involves some sort of exchange. This is true even in our relationship with God.

One of the most beautiful gifts God gives us is redemption. He exchanges one thing for something else. He restores. He rescues, and He frees us in a way no one else can.

When God put Adam and Eve in the garden of Eden, He had a perfect personal relationship with them. The Creator and the created were connected. When God gave them only one rule (not to eat of the tree of good and evil) and they broke that rule, their relationship with God was broken. With that one wrong choice, sin entered into this world. That sin now separated the Creator from the created. (You can read that story in the book of Genesis, chapters one through three.) Throughout the Old Testament, we see God's efforts to restore relationship with humankind through an established law and required sacrifices. (The Old Testament is the first part of the Bible. It is God's story before Jesus lived on this earth.) Before God sent His Son, Jesus, to earth, unholy people could not have a personal relationship with a Holy God.

In the New Testament, we see how God, out of His incredible love for us, sent His Son, Jesus, to this earth to be the final, perfect sacrifice.

John 3:16 tells us this: "For God loved the world so much that he gave his one and only Son, so that everyone who believes in him will not perish but have eternal life" (NLT). God sent His Son to this earth, in part to be a living demonstration of how to live, but most importantly to live a sinless life and then die on a cross in our place. His life was exchanged for ours. That is why Jesus is called our "Redeemer."

However, God will never force Himself on us. He wants a personal relationship with us, in which we interact with Him on a regular basis. It's not about going to church. Church attendance isn't what puts us in relationship with God. I love what Billy Sunday once said: "Going to church doesn't make you a Christian any more than going to a garage makes you an automobile." Being part of a church family is something we do to stay connected to God and to stay connected to other believers. It is important. However, it's not what establishes us in a personal relationship with God.

Jesus exchanged His perfect life for imperfect lives.

You see, God reaches out His hand, inviting us to grab it and say yes to Him. You can do that in church on a Sunday morning, or you can do that sitting here with this book in your hands. God wants a friendship with you. Jesus exchanged His perfect life for our imperfect lives. He saved us from a life spent apart from God. That's why He is called "Savior."

If you have never said yes to God, you can do that now by praying these words or something similar to them: *God, I want to know You. I want my identity to be determined by You and only You. Thank You for sending Jesus to this earth. I accept Him as my Savior, and I want Him to be the leader of my life. Today I'm grabbing Your hand that's reaching out to me. In Jesus' name, amen.*

If you prayed that prayer for the very first time, I want you to email me and tell me! (You'll find my email at the back of the book.) Just put "I said Yes!" in the subject line so I'll make sure to see it and celebrate with you! If you said yes to God a while ago, let this be your reminder of the beautiful exchange God made for you. He's in the redemption business, but not just once in our lives. God continues to redeem. That means He forgives the past and gives us a future. The Bible tells us He says He will exchange beauty for ashes (Isaiah 61:3). This means God can make something beautiful out of the broken places in our lives.

One of my favorite verses in the Bible is Joel 2:25, where God says He will redeem what the locusts have eaten. This means He will restore our lives after devastation. We don't have to worry about plagues of locusts in this day and age, but there are other "plagues" that cause damage in our lives. Have you ever been plagued with worry over a wayward child? Have you been plagued with resentment over a broken relationship? Have you been plagued with guilt when you did something you shouldn't have done or said something you shouldn't have said? Have you been plagued with pain after someone you love has betrayed your trust? God longs to redeem those hurt places. He wants to exchange them for something new. He wants to restore and renew the broken places in our lives.

I've experienced God's redemption in my life, and I am so grateful. When our daughter Erica turned fourteen, we launched into the hardest four years of our parenting. Erica rejected her faith and family in so many ways. It was exhausting to parent her. She married at eighteen and shortly thereafter began re-engaging in her faith journey as her

....

husband, Kendall, began his own relationship with God. When Kendall was deployed to Iraq for a year, she asked if she could move home. Mark and I thought long and hard about having her home for a year, but we chose to say yes.

Partway through her year home, I started calling this our "bonus year." Erica was a joy to be around. We were enjoying this new relationship with our young adult, married daughter. The prodigal was home, and we saw firsthand how God was redeeming what the locusts had eaten.

I love the story of Joseph in the Bible. Joseph was one of the youngest of twelve sons and his father's favorite. Joseph's father gave him a special coat that was made of many different colors of material. Joseph's brothers were jealous of him, so they decided to first throw him in a pit and then sell him as a slave. They told their father Joseph had been killed by a wild animal.

Years went by, and Joseph experienced terrible things. He was a slave. He was falsely accused and imprisoned. He seemed to be forgotten by the world. But God had other plans. God chose to redeem the years the locusts had eaten in Joseph's life. God eventually not only gets Joseph out of prison, but He establishes him as the right-hand man to the pharaoh. Joseph's wisdom saves Egypt from being ruined during a seven-year drought. In an interesting turn of events, Joseph's brothers eventually come to Egypt begging for help (although they have no idea the man they are pleading with is really their brother!). I love what Joseph eventually says to his brothers: "You intended to harm me, but God intended it all for good. He brought me to this position so I could save the lives of many people" (Genesis 50:20 NLT).

....

God longs to bring restoration to your life and mine. He wants to use our experiences for His purposes. He can take the bad in our lives and make something good out of it. I've experienced this personally, too. I don't believe for one minute that God wanted my husband to leave our home. I believe God grieved right along with me while Mark wandered in his own personal desert. However, I can tell you that God used that hard season in my life for good. For starters, God greatly increased my compassion for hurting people. I'm such a black-and-white thinker that, before this heartbreak, I used to have very little compassion for others. My heart now breaks when I learn another person is hurting. Second, God increased my ability to empathize with others. I know what it feels like to be betrayed and deeply wounded. I can now better relate to the feelings others are experiencing in similar situations. Third, God grew my love for the Bible to a whole new level when I had to depend on it to get me through days when I just wanted to crawl in bed and wish the world away. God used a very difficult situation to draw me closer to Him and His Word.

Do you have some broken places in your life that you'd like God to use for good? Are you ready to exchange your ashes for beauty? He's ready, willing, and able if you'll simply allow Him to do His best work!

WHAT WILL YOU DO?

You and I are now intricately aware of the symptoms of the Perfection Infection. We're now better equipped to identify the warning signs of this cultural epidemic. We've also been entrusted with the antidotes that can begin to eradicate the disease that has divided mothers for far too long.

I love the perspective one seasoned friend shared about the Perfection Infection: "The older I get, the closer I get to figuring out that there is no enviable life out there. I need to pay more attention to the blessings I have and less to the myopic illusion that others are better, and better off, than I am." What a beautiful way to summarize the essence of this book.

The question is, What will you do now? Will you continue as you did before you were aware? Will you keep on spreading the disease? Will you simply hope someone else in your circle of influence will take that first step?

With hope, I'd like to ask you to consider these four responses:

1. *Will you determine you'll never be the same* now that you see how much damage the Perfection Infection inflicts on our lives, our families, and our friendships?
2. *Will you be part of the solution* by carrying the cure into your circle of influence and applying the antidotes as often as you can?
3. *Will you commit* to be the best mom you can be without imposing unrealistic expectations on yourself and others?
4. *Will you embrace a new picture* of real motherhood and share it with others? It would include:

No expectations.
    No pride.
        No fear.
            No insecurity.
                No judgment.
                    No comparisons.

· · · · · · · ·

No agenda.

No performing.

No more perfect moms . . .

. . . just imperfect moms partnering with a perfect God.

THIS IS *Who I Am*
IN GOD'S EYES!

I am faithful (Ephesians 1:1).

I am God's child (John 1:12).

I am Christ's friend (John 15:15).

I belong to God (1 Corinthians 6:20).

I am assured all things work together for good (Romans 8:28).

I am confident that God will perfect the work He has begun in me (Philippians 1:6).

I am a citizen of heaven (Philippians 3:20).

I have not been given a spirit of fear, but of power, love, and self-discipline (2 Timothy 1:7).

I am born of God, and the evil one cannot touch me (1 John 5:18).

I am chosen before the creation of the world (Ephesians 1:4, 11).

I am adopted as God's child (Ephesians 1:5).

I am given God's glorious grace lavishly and without restriction (Ephesians 1:5, 8).

I am forgiven (Ephesians 1:7; Colossians 1:14).

I have purpose (Ephesians 1:9; 3:11).

I have hope (Ephesians 1:18).

I have been chosen (Ephesians 1:3–4).

I am God's coworker (2 Corinthians 6:1).

I have been shown the incomparable riches of God's grace (Ephesians 2:7).

God has expressed His kindness to me (Ephesians 2:7).

I am God's workmanship (Ephesians 2:10).

I have peace (Ephesians 2:14).

I have access to the Father (Ephesians 2:18).

I am a member of God's household (Ephesians 2:19).

I am secure (Ephesians 2:20).

I am a dwelling for the Holy Spirit (Ephesians 2:22).

God's power works through me (Ephesians 3:7).

I can approach God with freedom and confidence (Ephesians 3:12).

I know there is a purpose for my sufferings (Ephesians 3:13).

I am completed by God (Ephesians 3:19).

I can be humble, gentle, patient, and lovingly tolerant of others (Ephesians 4:2).

I can mature spiritually (Ephesians 4:15).

I can have a new attitude and a new lifestyle (Ephesians 4:21–32).

I can be kind and compassionate to others (Ephesians 4:32).

I can forgive others (Ephesians 4:32).

I can understand what God's will is (Ephesians 5:17).

I can give thanks for everything (Ephesians 5:20).

I don't have to always have my own agenda (Ephesians 5:21).

I can honor God through marriage (Ephesians 5:22–33).

I can parent my children with composure (Ephesians 6:4).

I can be strong (Ephesians 6:10).

I have God's power (Ephesians 6:10).

I can stand firm against evil (Ephesians 6:13).

I am not alone (Hebrews 13:5).

I am growing (Colossians 2:7).

I am united with other believers (John 17:20–23).

I am not in want (Philippians 4:19).

I am promised eternal life (John 6:47).

I am chosen and dearly loved (Colossians 3:12).

I am blameless (1 Corinthians 1:8).

I am set free (Romans 8:2; John 8:32).

I am a light in the world (Matthew 5:14).

I am more than a conqueror (Romans 8:37).

I am safe (1 John 5:18).

I am part of God's kingdom (Revelation 1:6).

I am no longer condemned (Romans 8:1–2).

I am not helpless (Philippians 4:13).

I am protected (John 10:29).

I am born again (1 Peter 1:23).

I am a new creation (2 Corinthians 5:17).

I am delivered (Colossians 1:13).

I am victorious (1 Corinthians 15:57; 1 John 5:4).

⋆──────⋆

Compiled by Beth Bolthouse, M.A., LPC
www.lifeinvestmentnetwork.com. Used with permission.

WHERE TO FIND HELP
WHEN *Feeling*...

Angry	Ephesians 4:26–27, 31–32; Colossians 3:7–8, 12–17
Bitter	1 Corinthians 13; Hebrews 12:14–15; Ephesians 4:31–32
Bored	1 Thessalonians 5:16, 18; Philippians 4:8; Ephesians 5:15–16; Psalm 34:1
Critical	Matthew 7:1–5; Romans 1:32–2:1; James 4:11–12
Defeated	Romans 8:31–39; Philippians 4:13; 1 Peter 1:6–7; 1 Peter 5:7
Depressed	Psalm 34; Psalm 37; 2 Corinthians 4:7–10, 16–18; Matthew 11:28

Disappointed	Psalm 16:11; Jeremiah 29:11–13; Philippians 4:19; John 14:1
Disbelief	Mark 9:24; 2 Timothy 2:13; Hebrews 11:6; John 14:1
Discouraged	Psalm 23; Psalm 42:6–11; Psalm 55:22; Matthew 5:11–12
Dishonest	Proverbs 12:22; Jeremiah 7:8–10; 1 Thessalonians 4:6; John 8:32
Doubt	Numbers 23:19; Matthew 8:26; John 14:1; Proverbs 3:5–6
Embarrassed	Psalm 27:1–3; Psalm 34, Psalm 35; Colossians 3:1–2; Psalm 23
Fear	Psalm 34:4; Matthew 10:28; 2 Timothy 1:7; Hebrews 13:5–6
Guilty	1 John 1:9; Psalm 51; Psalm 103; Hebrews 10:17; Romans 8:1
Hatred	Proverbs 10:12; 1 John 2:9–11; 1 John 3:10–15; 1 John 4:20
Hypocritical	Luke 6:46; Titus 1:16; 1 Peter 2:1; Ephesians 4:1
Immoral	1 Peter 2:11; Galatians 5:16; 2 Timothy 2:22; Psalm 51
Impatient	Psalm 25:5; Psalm 27:14; Habakkuk 2:3; Psalm 37:34
Judgmental	Matthew 7:1–5; Luke 6:37
Lonely	Psalm 23; Psalm 68:6; Hebrews 13:5–6; Jeremiah 23:23; Matthew 28:20

Lazy	Romans 12:11; Ephesians 5:15–16; Hebrews 6:12; Proverbs 6:6–11
Overwhelmed	Psalm 46:1; Psalm 50:15; Proverbs 11:8; James 1:2–3
Persecuted	2 Timothy 3:12: John 15:20; Acts 14:22: Hebrews 12:3
Pressured	Isaiah 26:3; 2 Chronicles 16:9; Philippians 4:13; 2 Timothy 1:7
Prideful	Proverbs 16:18; 1 Corinthians 10:12; Philippians 2:3; James 4:6
Revengeful	Proverbs 17:13; Romans 12:16–19; 1 Peter 2:23
Sad	Isaiah 14:3; Romans 8:28; Revelation 21:4; Isaiah 35:10
Slandered	Psalm 15:1–3; Matthew 5:11–12; Matthew 12:36; 1 Corinthians 4:13
Suicidal	Luke 4:9–12; Genesis 28:15; 2 Peter 2:9; Psalm 23
Ungrateful	Psalm 69:30; Ephesians 5:20; 1 Thessalonians 5:18; 1 Timothy 2:1
Unloved	Jeremiah 31:3; Romans 5:8; 1 John 4:8–19; Lamentations 3:22–23
Weak	Isaiah 40:29–31; 1 Corinthians 12:9; 2 Timothy 1:7; Philippians 4:13
Worry	Matthew 6:19–34; Luke 12:25–26; Philippians 4:6–7; Psalm 23
Worthless	1 Samuel 16:7: Psalm 139:13–15; John 10:3; Jeremiah 31:3

. . . .

Acknowledgments

No book is written in isolation. This message emerges from my personal experiences and the experiences of thousands of moms I have encouraged over the past twenty years. With that in mind, I want to express my appreciation to:

Every mom who has shared her story, frustrations, joys, and discoveries with me. Each story has helped formulate the message of this book.

The beautiful people who make up the Hearts at Home leadership team. It is a joy to serve with such a wonderful group of men and women.

My mom-in-the-trenches readers who gave valuable initial feedback: Becky, Bonnie, Kelly, Megan, Angie, Anne, and Erica. Your willingness to read some or all of the chapters as they were being created was so important!

My prayer team: Thank you for standing in the gap for me! Your time on your knees is more important a contribution to this book than any words I write.

The Moody Publishers team: Deb Keiser, Michele Forrider, Janis Backing, Holly Kisly. Thank you for believing in the message of this book! Thank you, Annette LaPlaca, for strengthening the message with your wonderful editing skills!

Anne, Evan, Erica, Kolya, and Austin: Thank you for allowing me to share your stories. You're the best kids a mom could ask for!

Mark: I love how God is rewriting our love story.

God: Thank You for loving this imperfect mom so perfectly.

Dear Reader,

I'd love to hear how this book has encouraged you personally! You can email me at jillannsavage@yahoo.com. You can also find me on Facebook (Jill Fleener Savage) and Twitter (jillsavage).

Make sure you check out the No More Perfect Moms website at www. NoMorePerfectMoms.com, where you'll find additional resources to encourage you and to equip you to lead a book study, if you desire.

You'll also find more encouragement at:

❧ My blog and website: www.jillsavage.org

❧ Hearts at Home website: www.hearts-at-home.org

Joining you in the journey,

Jill

HEARTS
at HOME

The Go-To Place for Moms

*H*earts at Home's mission is to encourage, educate, and equip every mom in every season of motherhood using Christian values to strengthen families. Founded in 1993, Hearts at Home offers a variety of resources and events to assist women in their roles as wives and mothers.

Hearts at Home is designed to provide you with ongoing education and encouragement in your journey of motherhood. In addition to this book, our resources include the *Heartbeat* radio program and our extensive Hearts at Home website, blog, and eCommunity. We also offer a monthly free eNewsletter called Hearts On-The-Go as well as daily encouragement on Facebook and Twitter.

Additionally, Hearts at Home conference events make a great getaway for individuals, moms' groups, or for enjoying time with that special friend, sister, or sister-in-law. The regional conferences, attended by more than nine thousand women each year, provide a unique, affordable, and highly encouraging weekend for any mom in any season of motherhood.

Hearts at Home
1509 N. Clinton Blvd.
Bloomington, IL 61701
Phone: (309) 828-MOMS
E-mail: hearts@hearts-at-home.org
Web: www.hearts-at-home.org

. . . .

*A*lmost every mom does it.

We love our children so much and we wrestle with our parenting decisions so strenuously that we tend to defend our personal choices too ferociously.

"I can't believe she's using formula."
"Can you believe she's going back to work?"
"How can she send her kids to public school?"
"She's throwing away her degree staying home."
"How are they affording that *college?"*

That's how the mommy wars started.

However, this is a war that can't be won. The constant battles divide us from the very women we need in our lives.

Hearts at Home believes it's time for a call to action:

KNOCK IT OFF!

That's what we tell our kids when we want them to stop fighting, so that's what we're calling moms to do, too.

Embrace differences.

Stop judging yourself.

Stop judging each other.

Replace criticism with grace.

Put down the stone and pick up the phone.

Will you join us?

Make your commitment count at www.KnockItOffMoms.com!

· · · · · · · ·

*L*ooking to strengthen your resolve to love your real life?

Do you have an imperfect mom story you'd like to share?

Want to share the *No More Perfect Mom* book and experience with other moms?

Looking for a leader's guide or discussion videos to use in your moms group?

Want to put an "I'm an Imperfect Mom and That's Okay" button on your blog or Facebook page?

You'll find it all online at
www.NoMorePerfectMoms.com

Come hang out with other imperfect moms who are learning to love their real lives!